Enjoy Life!
Healing with Happiness

How to Harness Positive Moods to Raise
Your Energy, Effectiveness, and Joy

By Lynn D. Johnson, Ph.D.

D0957290

Published by
Head Acre Press
166 East 5900 South, Suite B-108
Salt Lake City, UT 84107, U.S.A.

Copyright © 2008 Lynn D. Johnson

Library of Congress Cataloging-in-Publication Data
Johnson, Lynn D.
Enjoy Life: Healing With Happiness
Includes biliographical references.
ISBN: 978-0-9762734-1-7
1. Happiness. 2. Personal effectiveness 1.Title

Printed in the United States of America
1   3   5   7   9   10   8   6   4   2

If you have purchased the print edition or the digital edition this book via the
internet, as a registered user, you are entitled to recent updates. Email
Updates@enoylifebook.com and download your materials. New information will be
added from time to time.

In gratitude to the
Committee for Better Times Book Club
and their help in reading and finding my
many mistakes.
Thanks, Ann, Liz, Lorna, and Sally.
Good eye! Your work was indispensable.
Thanks, Julie. Thanks, Debbie.

Thanks to my dear wife, Carol Sue who tolerated
hours of absence and made so many helpful suggestions.

Thanks to those who suggested titles and cover designs.

Without all of you, this book would not be possible

Contents

Introduction

My friend Frank and his charming wife Sarah were giving me a tour around Washington, D.C., when we heard the news. Some terrorists had tried to smuggle bomb-making chemicals disguised in drink containers onto an airplane in London. New emergency rules had gone into effect, and the news was that airport security had slowed to a crawl all over the country. I was worried. Would I miss my plane home because of this crisis? I cut short the tour, and Sarah dropped me off at a subway station.

I descended into the Metro tunnel and paid my fare. There was a square post that showed the Metro lines that stopped at that station. I wanted the train that went to Crystal City, across the Potomac. Staring at the post, I learned that the Blue line went to Crystal City and Reagan National Airport. But I was confused. All the lines were parallel, and the next three trains that came through the station were not Blue trains. Where was my train?

Impatient to do *something*, I struggled with a temptation to get on one of the parallel lines. They looked like they were going to similar places. So

I pulled out my Metro D.C. map and learned that each line was not parallel. They looked parallel on the post, but that was misleading. The Green and Red lines went to completely different parts of the city. Calming my anxiety, I resolved to wait for the right train.

Finally a Blue train arrived, I entered and sat down, able to relax and enjoy the ride across the river and past the Pentagon. It occurred to me that we all have trains of thought that come rumbling through our awareness and in our anxiety we are tempted to get onto the first one. We may have too much trust in the first train of thought that rolls into our consciousness. Clearly it is going *somewhere*.

But does that train stop anywhere you want to go? Since I needed a particular stop, it made no sense to get onto the first train. In fact, to fall to that temptation would have guaranteed my most feared future – missing my airplane – coming true.

We want to get to happiness. Psychologists now know that happy people are more productive, more creative. They give more to charity and volunteer to give blood and mark their drivers licenses as being organ donors. They are easier to work with and be married to. Habitually happy people are simply better citizens. And it is the habitual trains of thought that the happy people get on that takes them to habitual happiness.

How often do we get onto a train of thought that will not take us where we want to go? I watched a mother and son arguing one day, and when they looked to me ("You're the shrink, earn your pay!") I pointed out that each of them was on a train of thought that would not end well. There were no stops on that line that they wanted. The each needed a change of heart. They needed a different train of thought.

What if there were some easy, natural ways for you to identify the right train of thought for yourself? What if you can heal life's pain with that right train? What if taking the right train were as simple as waiting for it to come by?

The new field of Positive Psychology was the inspiration for this book. I wrote it because I have been giving classes and workshops on Positive Psychology. I wanted to share with students what we are learning about joy and happiness.

Happiness is a new direction for shrinks. We have mostly been interested in what is wrong with people, why they get depressed, anxious, and into conflicts with people they love. We study anger and fear and try to make people better. But traditionally we have not studied hope, love, inspiration, and joy.

What a shame. We want to live lives of joy and fulfillment. In fact, when we look at young children, it is clearly our natural state, a "default setting" to use today's computer lingo. Through research into high functioning people, we now know that people high in curiosity are much happier. And curiosity is the most natural state possible. Young children are full of curiosity, wanting to know and learn. If you want to be a happier person, all you have to do is remember that natural curiosity.

Imagine a group of people asked to write down an ideal day, one that would surely make them happy. What might be on the list? Often people write down things that would give them enjoyment and pleasure. Maybe some exciting things are on the list, maybe some relaxing ones. Perhaps one person would ride roller-coasters, or perhaps another would spend the day at a spa, getting facials, massages, being around scented candles, or relaxing. Some would spend part of an ideal day in a beautiful natural environment, like high in the mountains, or at the seashore. Another might be an excitement junkie, and an ideal day would be skydiving, driving race cars, riding mountain bikes down twisting wooded trails, or scuba diving on a mysterious shipwreck.

Generally we see a big shift from the typical day. Few people say, "Oh, I'd do what I did yesterday." It would be a change. That makes sense. We all like change, we all like seeing a new movie, not going to one we have seen before.

Actually, the things most people describe in their ideal day are things that bring pleasure and satisfaction or perhaps excitement and adventure, but not happiness, certainly not joy. There is a big difference. Pleasure is actually not strongly associated with joy. A small amount of pleasure or excitement is helpful, like a small amount of vitamin C will prevent scurvy. But more C doesn't seem to confer much additional benefit. I secretly believe in taking extra C, but when I look at the actual scientific studies, there is no evidence that I am right. Taking large doses didn't prevent colds or make them pass more quickly. What I believe isn't supported by the science. I hate it when science tells me I am wrong.

So it is with happiness. The things that we think will give us more happiness don't deliver. New cars, more money, fancy vacations, all fail to make us lastingly happy.

Let's take money. That's something everyone is interested in, and most people believe if they had $10,000 more a year, they would be happier. But the psychology research on that is pretty grim. People are temporarily happier when they get extra money. They have a temporary increase in excitement and pleasure. And then a cruel, cruel thing happens. They *habituate* to the new money. They get used to it very quickly. Their happiness level returns to the original level.

That process is called *the hedonic treadmill*. We run faster and faster and don't get any further. Habituation to pleasure led some psychologists to say that our happiness level is a fixed quantity, almost certainly determined by genetic factors, and it cannot be changed. As you will see, this turns out to not be true. There is much we can do. But it doesn't involve pleasure, excitement, fine homes or cars, status symbols, and the like.

Restoring or transforming?

My career as a psychologist involves taking a patient who is suffering from anxiety or depression and bringing her back to a normal range. Often I meet with someone whose marriage is in trouble and I help him get that marriage back on track. Let me illustrate with the charts on the next page.

The first vertical line represents some kind of trauma or setback. A

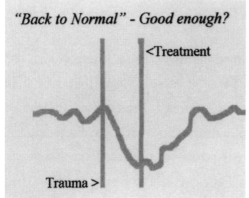

"Back to Normal" - Good enough?

person's spirits sink. They are depressed. The second line is where the person reaches out to get some help. Therapy helps them and they return to where they were before. Everyone is happy.

I am glad to have a job where I am helping people. But a return to normal isn't always enough. You see, people often relapse. They slide back into their depression, their anxiety states. Their marriage gets back into trouble again. What they need is not a return to their old state. What they need is a transformation.

There is a program on TV these days called "The Biggest Loser." It is an inspiring show about morbidly obese people, people more than 100 pounds overweight. Their health is endangered. Their lives are compromised. Their

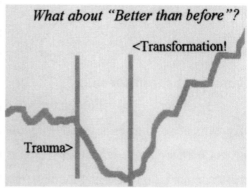

What about "Better than before"?

relationships are damaged. These are people who didn't want to be fat, but they became fat against their will, who have tried all kinds of diets but are unable to keep weight off.

In this television program, we see people losing over 100 pounds through a mix of healthy eating habits and rigorous exercise. The before-and-after pictures are amazing. If they can internalize this change of diet and increase in exercise, and make it permanent, they will have accomplished a miracle.

Treating depression or anxiety in the usual way is just returning people to their former state. We shrinks have done a fairly good job at that. We have some very effective methods of helping people achieve relief from many of the problems that disturb them. In treating depression, we have a good success rate. Around half or more of our patients make a full recovery from depression, for example, and another 20% or so make very good improvement. Frankly, those numbers are better than almost any other medical intervention for chronic health problems.

But it is not be enough. You see, people do relapse. They do fall back into their old problem. So while we restore people, we really need to transform them. We don't want the first graph, we want the second one.

That's what this book is about. A famous psychiatrist once said, "People are born princes and princesses, and their parents turn them into frogs. When they come to a psychiatrist, they don't want to be a prince or a princess. They just want to be a better adjusted frog." (Eric Berne.)

Well, in one way, I think Berne was wrong. The role of genes plays a part in people becoming frogs. We'll say more about that in the last chapter. Our society, the culture we live in, plays a part. Likely, even our diet plays a role. We no longer blame all problems on parents. But the spirit of the statement is correct. Our goals are too limited. We don't want to be deeply happy, just a bit happier. We don't want to be wildly successful, just a little successful. We don't want to be the greatest friend, spouse or parent, just a bit better.

We often don't even trust the notion of being significantly happier, as if there were something sinful about it. We just want to get rid of our acute pain, go back to our low-level chronic pain.

This book is not about that. It is about transformation.

What do you want to be? Frog or princess?

Lynn D. Johnson, Ph.D.
Salt Lake City, August 2008

Dealing with Downers:

Trading a Dark Mood for a Light One.

Here you find some keys to raising hope and optimism.

Chapter 1
How Happiness Went to the Dogs

Optimism is the faith that leads to achievement. Nothing can be done without hope and confidence.
– Helen Keller

M arty Seligman was interested in depression. As a graduate student in psychology, he found the common explanations for that illness shallow and unsatisfying. In his book, *Learned Optimism*, he describes how he stumbled onto an observation about lab dogs who appeared depressed. They had been the subjects of a training experiment that involved punishment. When they made a mistake in learning the skill, they received a brief electric shock. But instead of learning what the experimenter wanted them to learn, they just laid in their cages and whined.

Seligman thought they looked like depressed people. They were sad, they didn't get excited to play, they lost interest in food and seemed to not sleep well. But the behaviorist doctrine of the time said that dogs couldn't be depressed. They didn't have a language and the intellect of humans, so it was impossible to say they had human feelings. Seligman wasn't so sure.

Is it Ethical to Experiment on Animals?

He did some soul searching. Should he experiment with dogs, with the intent of making them depressed? This would cause suffering. Was he justified? After discussing it with trusted advisors, he decided that he was justified, if he was likely to relieve more suffering in the world by what he learned. He hated the idea of causing the dogs to suffer. But he hated the suffering people experience from depression even more.

His experiment consisted of two sets of dogs who received harmless but painful electric shocks. One set could do something to end the shocks, but the other set could do nothing. They were helpless. If the dogs thought they could end the shocks, such as by jumping over a barrier, they did not get depressed. They thought they had power. But the helpless dogs did get depressed. They didn't want to play with the experimenter. They whined and laid around and didn't want to eat or play with other dogs.

Two things could help the dogs. First, if they were given a dog-sized dose of an antidepressant, they perked up and seemed to feel quite a bit better. Second, if the experimenter taught them that they were not helpless. When he dragged them over the barrier and showed them again and again how that would stop the shock, they became active again. It was as if they had learned to have hope that they could influence their world.

There's Nothing I Can Do

Seligman called his theory the "learned helplessness" model. Behaviorists were outraged. They thoroughly chastised him. "Dogs don't learn concepts, they learn behavior," they argued. "You cannot attribute higher level thinking to them." But in a series of experiments Seligman showed that there was no other explanation that made sense.

Dogs can have hope or despair in their hearts. If they view themselves as helpless, they feel despair when something bad happens.

Dogs were thinking creatures, trying to figure out the world and their place in it. Dogs could have hope or despair in their hearts. If they viewed themselves as helpless, they felt despair when something bad happened. The dogs who could never escape the punishment thought of themselves as helpless. The word in their heart was "no." The other dogs, the active ones, were able to jump a barrier to stop the painful shock. Bad things happened, but they saw themselves as able to stop the badness. If they had hope, if they thought they were powerful, then when bad things happened, they never quit trying. The word in their heart was "yes."

Both dogs got exactly the same electric shocks. When the dog in the active condition jumped the barrier, the other dog's shock instantly stopped too. The difference was that one *made it happen*, whereas the other dog was passive, the shock just stopped. The dog that jumps, the dog that is active is not emotionally harmed by the shock. The second dog, the powerless dog did become depressed. Having no power creates depression.

Its Not What Happens to You

The dogs' general attitude about the world was what made the difference, not whether the next experiment they were subjected to involved punishment and pain. All the dogs suffered the exact same amount of pain. The active condition dogs were *resilient*, that is, they weren't defeated by a punishing experience. The dogs in the passive condition were vulnerable. They had been taught that they were helpless. They were set back by the same punishments. They would become depressed when in a punishing experiment that didn't bother the resilient dogs.

Life does involve stress. Studies of people who are happier than average have shown that they do not have fewer painful experiences. They still suffer setbacks, failures, and disappointments. Singer-songwriter John Gorka says: "Life is full of disappointments, yes, and I am full of life." Pain is an unavoidable part of life. If you consistently develop resiliency it will not eliminate the pain of life. You will have pain. But you won't suffer.

A good rule: Pain is inevitable. Suffering is optional.

What we learn from Seligman's brilliant dog experiments is that suffering is separate from pain. We all feel pain. But how much does that pain bother us? How much must we suffer? It depends entirely on our own resiliency.

The Keys to Optimism

Again we go to Seligman, a deep well of wisdom. In England he was presenting his theory of learned helplessness. He had graduated from dogs and was now into making volunteer humans depressed, by putting them into painful experiences from which they could not escape. He learned his dog experiments translated directly to understanding human depression. The groups of experimental subjects who were in the "learned helplessness condition" and couldn't take a step to end the pain did shift into clinical depression. They had learned that they were helpless, and then when a pain came, they became depressed.

Seligman read his latest paper to a group of scholars at the English clinic, Tavistock, a famous psychology center in London.

In the front row of professors and students sat a man who kept frowning and shaking his head in disagreement. Seligman wondered if he were an old behaviorist upset about the thinking orientation of his explanations. As he sat down, the moderator said, "Now Professor Teasdale will discuss Professor Seligman's paper. The frowner stood up and came to the rostrum.

"Professor Seligman's theory tells us nothing," claimed Teasdale. "Not all the people in his experiments became depressed. Unless he can explain why some of them do not become depressed, he cannot explain anything." Seligman realized that Teasdale was correct. Some dogs didn't seem to learn that they were helpless. Some people seemed impervious to his learned helplessness experiments.

Seligman sought out Teasdale and found to his delight that his critic actually had some ideas about how to understand why some people are resilient. Teasdale was working on the concept that how we explain the world is a stable and enduring feature. Some

> *Optimists think bad things are **temporary** and good things are **permanent**. Pessimists believe the opposite.*

people's explanation for bad events, for example, is that they will be *permanent*, they will expect bad to last a long time. They are vulnerable to becoming depressed when they suffer a painful experience. Other people expect bad events to last a short time, they are *temporary*. So when the same painful experience occurs, they are still hopeful. "Oh," they say, "never mind, it will pass quickly."

Seligman and Teasdale worked out three types of attributions people make. Events can be (1) *permanent* or *temporary*. They can be (2) *personally caused* or *impersonal* or something that just happens, a meaningless accident. And they can be (3) *pervasive*, that is, they will affect every part of one's life, or they can be *local*, meaning they affect one part of life but not others.

Healthy Inconsistency

They found something very interesting. The most resilient people were inconsistent. When a good thing happened, the healthy, resilient people said, "That is permanent (lasting a long time), it is personal (caused by me), and it is pervasive (affects many parts of my life)." But then when a bad thing happened, the resilient person said, "It is temporary (pass quickly), it is impersonal (it just happened, I didn't really cause it), and it is local and won't affect other parts of my life."

But let's not criticize the resilient people. The most fragile people who are prone to depression are also inconsistent! They believe the mirror

> *Angels fly because they take themselves lightly.*
> – G. K. Chesterton

opposite: A bad event? It is permanent, it is personally caused, and it is pervasive. But a good experience? Now that is a horse of a different color. A good event is temporary. It isn't caused by me, they say to themselves, but it is just something that randomly happens. And there is no sense in getting too excited, they think. It isn't going to affect other parts of my life.

It is almost as if Mother Nature is telling you, "Don't try to be consistent, you foolish human. You cannot. Just adopt a resilient inconsistency." That is, we can learn to be more resilient. When we do that, we become less prone to depression.

Seligman and his colleagues tried an experiment. They identified some grade school children who were at risk for depression. Half of the students

9

got a twelve week class on how to think more optimistically. They were taught to practice thinking of bad as temporary and not personal. They also learned to think of good things as permanent and personally caused. The next year, the treated group only had half of the episodes of depression as the untreated group. Is it worth a few weeks of classwork if we can reduce depression in the most vulnerable children by half?

It is clear from that series of experiments that happiness can be changed. We know now that happy people are more optimistic, and optimistic people are far less vulnerable to depression. They bounce back quickly from disasters. It has to do with their expectations. They expect good things to happen and they expect to avoid most bad things.

But this turns out to not be true. Many investigations have shown convincingly that bad events occur to happy people just as often as to unhappy people. Pain occurs in each life. There is no escaping it. The difference is the explanations. So it turns out that it really isn't what happens to you that creates your reactions. It is all about what you think about the bad and the good experiences. It is about how you explain events.

Reflect on the fact that we were optimistic as children. We hoped good things would happen, we could get into arguments with our little friends but we didn't let angry feelings stay with us. We got over it quickly. Bad things were temporary. And we tended not to blame ourselves for bad events. They just happened, and we could bounce back quickly from them. To a certain extent, being optimistic as an adult is simply remembering what we originally knew.

But sometimes we need more than to just remember how we were as children. We need some simple, and hopefully easy activities we can do to bring back that optimism. We need to remember who we were originally, and get back to that childlike optimism. We will discuss that in the next chapter on Learning Optimism.

What have we covered?

● Depression is caused by the belief that one is helpless.

● When a painful event occurs, the pessimistic person becomes depressed. Pessimism makes people vulnerable. Pain makes them depressed.

● Optimism prevents depression. It is made of three general attitudes about the world:

  • Good things last a long time, bad passes quickly

  • Good events are caused by me, bad just happens.

  • Good stuff spreads, bad experiences are limited.

TRY THIS: Take Seligman's Optimism test. Go to his website at www.authentichappiness.org and register (for free!). There are many interesting tests you can take. For now, take his optimism test and write about the results in your diary. Maybe you will take it again in three months and find to your delight that your optimism has increased. Bear in mind that, with the exception of attorneys, optimism predicts greater success in every area of life. Only attorneys have to bear the burden of pessimism. The rest of us can increase our joy and increase our success. We can return to our natural inheritance of optimism that we had as children.

Would you like more information, extra insights I couldn't put into the book, or new developments? If you bought a hard copy of the book, or if you are a registered user of the E-book, you are entitled to that info. Send an Email to:
Updates@enjoylifebook.com
You will get a reply telling you how to download new materials.

Chapter 2
Learning Optimism

*"I can't change the direction of the wind, but
I can always adjust my sails to reach my
destination."*
– Jimmy Dean

The good news is that we can learn to be more optimistic. When I was living in Argentina, I tried hard to master the Spanish language. I felt good about how much I did learn, although it was far from fluent. I met an older woman, a British woman in her sixties, who didn't speak any Spanish at all, though she had lived in Argentina for over thirty years, arriving as a newlywed with her husband.

Another older lady I met was from Russia. She spoke Russian, French, German, and Spanish, as well as some English. A fascinating person, she was always interested in learning new things. She also had been in Argentina for some thirty years, and in that time she had mastered the new language and was quite fluent.

One learned, another didn't. The key was simply in how much effort they each put into the new language. I will let you guess which woman was a happier person, and which I preferred to visit with.

Looking back, I believe the Russian woman was like the resilient dogs that Seligman studied. She had learned that what she did made a difference, and so she put in the effort to master new languages. She was optimistic.

That is the key to optimism. One person will read this book and think, "I could never learn to be optimistic." Of course, that person is right. He cannot do it.

A second person reads this book, a pessimistic and unhappy person, and she thinks, "This is important. I need to do this. Even if I don't think I can, it is important that I try." So she starts to practice optimism and before long she is much more optimistic. She can do it.

The only difference is the amount of practice. It is not talent. It is not intelligence or good looks. It is certainly not an expensive education. We find practice is the only factor that differentiates successful from unsuccessful people. The successful people have engaged in deliberate practice. They find out what to practice, usually from someone who is a coach or teacher. They consistently put in more time and effort. They have an ongoing relationship with their coach, who corrects them and gives them new skills to practice.

Practice, not Talent

K. Anders Ericcson is a professor at Florida State University, where he studies high performance. He found that the average pianist had practiced around 2000 hours by the time he or she was twenty years old. The concert pianists who went on to play at the top levels had practiced around 10,000 hours – five times more practice. Early talent didn't predict anything about who would be a wonderful musician. Only the amount of practice lets us

> *It is not the athletically talented child who will become the basketball or football star, it is the child who practices the most. It is not the smartest person in the room who becomes the world famous surgeon, but the one who works the longest and hardest.*

predict. Ericsson has shown that effect in every area of human excellence. It is not the athletically talented child who will become the basketball or football star, it is the child who practices the most. It is not the smartest person in the room who becomes the world famous surgeon or physicist or writer, it is the one who works the longest and hardest.

So some will read this and not practice the skills. Others will. Those who do will permanently change their happiness levels for the better. Those who read and move on will not be helped.

Which one will you be?

How to Practice Optimism

Let's make this simple. It wouldn't be a bad idea to start a simple diary. Using your diary, you can practice changing your thinking about good and bad experiences by writing about them in your diary.

When a bad event happens, write about it in your diary. Now write about the following:

- What will be the first sign that this event is no longer affecting me? How will I know I have bounced back? (This addresses the Permanence factor.)

- What evidence do I have that this bad event is just something that happens to people, and isn't necessarily all my fault? If it happened to others, would I blame them as I blame myself? (Personally caused factor.)

- What can I do today to start to bounce back from this? If it hadn't happened, what would I be doing in other areas of my life? (Pervasiveness.)

Now also write down the mirror image of those questions when a good thing happens. Shift your thinking toward resiliency by finding reasons why good things will last a long time, will help you in other areas, and are caused by you.

- How long will the good effects from this last? How can I keep the good effects going longer in my life? (Permanence.)

- How did I help this happen? What did I do right? (Personally caused.)

- How can I celebrate this with others? How can I "leverage" this good event in other areas of my life? (Pervasiveness.)

The Future Diary

Sonja Lyubomirsky has reported good results from asking people to write a diary about how they hope and expect their lives to go. When I read about that, I recalled my old teacher, Milton Erickson who would put clients into a deep trance and ask them to experience their problem as if it were completely resolved. He found that people who had the experience of the problem being solved tended to find ways to actually solve it. It is as if having a taste of success makes you move toward it.

Optimistic people expect good from the world. Writing about it regularly helps you to experience that ahead of time. Like previews of a movie you would like to see, you feel energized to make that outcome happen.

When I was writing my first book, *Psychotherapy in the Age of Accountability*, I would often get tired of working on it. To keep myself motivated, I would imagine I was holding the book. I would look at the cover, thumb through the pages. I would look at my own name on the cover. I would imagine giving the book to my relatives and friends.

This raised my motivation, increased my optimism ("I can, I will finish this book!") and resulted in success. And it was a success. The book was published, and literally dozens of people bought it! Not just my mother! <grin, wink>

Try the future diary. Write about your preferred future. What will it look like? What will you hear from other people in this positive future? What will you feel? How will your life change? How will this change influence other people? How will your positive future benefit other people?

17

Savoring

Some of my patients have found relief from discouragement and low energy by using this exercise of savoring.

Zest makes life better. Zestful people simply enjoy things more than people low in zestfulness, so when we talk about increasing our habitual level of happiness (what some call the "happiness set point") then increasing our ability to feel zestful helps. It is true that zestfulness is almost certainly an innate, inherited trait. But in the past few years, we have discovered that many of these traits are quite changeable. We can increase zest if we wish to.

How do we do it? How do we go about enjoying the things around us? The skill of Savoring can increase our zest, since by paying attention to the pleasant things in our lives, we develop a greater sense of excitement about having them happen again. We enjoy and we eagerly anticipate.

Think of wine tasters. You have seen them sniffing the wine as they swirl it around in the glass, then swishing it around in their mouth. They are trying to sense every aspect of the wine. Their attention is totally focused on the moment, on how they can tune in to every molecule of taste. They are *savoring* the wine.

A Buddhist teacher, Thich Naht Hahn, encourages his students to concentrate fully as they chew their food, chewing slowly and thoroughly. This helps them enjoy the food more thoroughly, and he says they end up eating and needing less because they extract all the goodness from the food they eat. A simple glass of milk and a piece of bread seems like a feast to Hahn as he savors his food.

Psychologists studying happiness wonder, is *savoring* a key to raising levels of happiness and zest? I suggest that you try this experiment. Choose a simple pleasure that you might enjoy, like walking the dog, or sitting outside on a pleasant afternoon. As you experience that pleasure, focus your attention on the experience. What are the sights? Sounds? Physical sensations? What kinds of inner feelings - gratitude, wonder, appreciation, amusement - do you notice in yourself? Spend some time at that.

If you savor one experience each day, you will soon develop a nice habit. You will find that there are many small things you appreciate and value each day. You might notice that your zest and enjoyment of life increases by the simple act of savoring and appreciating. You create a virtuous cycle of noticing-appreciating-gratitude, which leads to more noticing of your own progress. The more we practice this virtuous cycle, the stronger the habit becomes.

The Gratitude Diary

Writing three to five things that you are grateful for *every day* is a great help. What went well? What would you like to see continue? Be sure to include things that you did, not just things that happened to you. It is unwise to overlook your own good behavior – far better to notice what you do right and celebrate that. (Some people have what I like to call Pathological Humility. They seem to resist any appreciation of themselves. I think that attitude takes humility to an extreme. Please include in your diary things you did right. If you have pathological humility, then perhaps you could think that since appreciating yourself will lead to you making more of a positive contribution to the lives of others, you owe it to them to write about your strengths and gifts.)

Several studies have found the gratitude diary to be one of the most powerful tools at raising happiness levels. Marty Seligman has shown in a comparison study that the simple gratitude diary was as powerful as either medication or psychotherapy in treating depression. Between savoring and gratitude, you reawaken the child-like glee you once felt toward life. It is a powerful healing practice.

Reframing From Bad to Good

Lately I am asking people to write down something that day that irritated or bothered them. It doesn't have to be a huge tragedy. Those don't happen all that often, thankfully. No, I simply ask them to write down some small item that irked them.

Now *reframe* that event. What I mean is, the event is what it is, but the meaning we attribute to it is like a frame we put around a picture. The picture is the same, but the impact it has on us is changed by the frame as well as by the picture itself. When we *reframe* an event, we look for something that is actually positive about the negative event.

So I want you to write an answer . . . or two or three . . . to this question about the irritating event: "And how is that also good?" Perhaps you can think of something you need to learn. Maybe you will find a way to turn the bad event to your advantage. It is possible that you can help others benefit from your experience.

Bear in mind that there are few unmixed blessings or tragedies in this world. Winning the lottery doesn't solve problems, it merely changes them. So also with bad events. John Walsh suffered the worst imaginable experience: his child was kidnaped and murdered. I cannot think of a worse thing. But he turned it into a blessing. He started a TV series, "America's Most Wanted." His show has caused over a thousand vicious criminals to be apprehended. So if he can make something good come from that catastrophe, surely we can create some hidden blessing in every painful event. Paradoxically, we can actually learn to be grateful for our unpleasant and painful experiences as well as the pleasant ones.

What have we covered?

● We can learn to be more optimistic by:

• Keeping a diary in which we write about both good and bad events. We write reasons why the good events will last, will spread, and are because of our own actions. We write reasons why bad events will pass quickly, are limited in their effect, and why we aren't completely to blame.

• Writing in our diary descriptions of our preferred future.

• Savoring positive experiences in detail.

• Keeping a *gratitude diary.*

• *Reframing* unpleasant events, finding the hidden blessing.

TRY THIS:

Make a point of mentioning some of the blessings you write about in your gratitude diary. Notice the effect it has on others when you do that. Notice whether it empowers you (strengthens the positive feeling) when you share with others.

Chapter 3
Activity and Happiness

"What seems to us as bitter trials are often blessings in disguise"
  – Oscar Wilde

My wife's twenty year high school reunion was coming up and she wanted to lose twenty pounds for the occasion. She asked me what might work, and I suggested running. "I hate to run," she said. Well, naturally. No sane person likes to run. Some people say they like to run, but ask them the key question. "If running made you old and fat instead of younger and thin, would you still do it?" No? Then clearly they like the effects of running more than the act itself.

Go Slow

So my wife and I started to walk thirty minutes every morning. In the middle of the walk, we ran for one minute. After a week of that we could run easily for a minute and a half. Then we ran twice in that walk, a minute or so each time. Gradually we built up until we were running for thirty to forty minutes every morning.

In the middle of the run, we'd run faster for a minute or so, as a little boost, an interval where we pushed our metabolism up high.

At her high school reunion, she looked great, and all her friends were jealous. (And, after all, why are we going to class reunions unless it is to make people jealous?) At the same time, she was noticeably more cheerful when she was doing that running. Can regular exercise make us happier?

Exercise and Mood

The bitter truth is that exercise does improve mood. In a variety of studies we find we can lift the mood of depressed or anxious people significantly with at least thirty minutes a day of vigorous exercise. Our bodies function best when we work them.

Depression is especially responsive to exercise. One of the triggers for depression is the elevation of the stress hormone cortisol. But a good workout reduces that stress hormone and increases good feelings from the endorphins that are released. The building hormone DHEA (dihydroepianderosterone, the body's recovery hormone) is released when we feel good. DHEA is our friend, and cortisol is our friend only if we have to fight cave bears and sabre-tooth tigers. Otherwise, it is simply hard on our bodies. Exercise reduces the cortisol.

Studies on exercise and mood have included children, college students, men in a weight loss program, middle aged women, older men and women. In older people, exercise prevents the brain from shrinking. Exercise works. It lifts our mood nicely. Weight lifting works well, and so does running, swimming, aerobics, vigorous sports . . . There is no doubt about it.

What Kind of Exercise Should We Start With?

Some people start exercising in the wrong way. They don't check with their doctor to see if they are healthy enough for exercise. A visit there will help you get a healthy start.

Follow what your doctor says. If the doc doesn't have a specific program, I would suggest you start with walking. It is something that can be done all year around. Many malls are open early in the winter for walking groups who don't want to slip and fall on icy sidewalks. It takes almost no equipment. Get a good pair of walking shoes and you are set. It is a sociable activity. You can generally find people in your neighborhood to walk with, and it will increase your range of friends.

What about running? LSD is the way I used to run . . . Long, Slow Distance – go far before you go fast. I would run the following pattern: Monday: short day. Tuesday: long day. Wednesday: Another short day, Thursday: Another long day. Friday? Big surprise: short. Saturday is the super-long day, which is the sum of the short and long day. I rested on Sunday. LSD running is six days a week, always resting one day and following that with a short day. The idea is to go further before you go faster.

So I used to run four miles on the short day, six to eight miles on the long day, and ten to twelve miles on Saturday. I felt great. But because of some football injuries, my knees developed arthritis and I had to give it up.

If you have knee problems, swimming and bicycling work really well. Low-impact aerobics work splendidly.

Anaerobic exercise is weight-bearing exercise like weight lifting, pushups, sit ups, chin ups, and so on. How do they affect mood? They seem to work as well as the aerobic exercises, in terms of lifting your mood, and they should be part of any workout program.

Set Moderately Challenging Goals

If you are a runner, see how well you can do in a 5k race, then set a goal to improve your time. Write it down and put the goal where you see it every day.

Set a goal to exercise a certain number of minutes each week. Again, write it down and celebrate when you exceed that goal. Faster, higher, stronger . . . make a goal and then achieve it.

Get with a Group

Exercising with others works. People who have a group of people to exercise with will stick with their programs better than people doing it alone. There is a reason that aerobics classes are popular. It feels better to be with a group.

What about starting a group? Organize a walking group, or pull together some friends and neighbors who like to cycle or who are interesting in a swimming club. Studies of very happy people show they are very involved with others, both intimately and socially. Hiking with your family, walking with your friends, do it with other people.

Make it Fun

Friendly competition can make it fun. If you are a runner, club runs can be a lot of fun, and often there is a friendly get-together after the run.

If you are a walker, take a camera and try to grab some interesting shots. Take a dog with you, if the dog is well trained and will heel with or without a leash.

See how many people you can get to smile at you as you pass. Try different things to get a smile.

Join fund-raising groups. People run and bike to raise money for good causes like curing breast cancer.

A colleague plays a brisk game of volleyball on his lunch hour. What can you talk your colleagues into during lunch? Join softball leagues, play pickup basketball, sign up for a racquetball tournament.

Ponder this question: How can I get more fit and have fun at the same time?

How much fun did you have the last time you exercised? Rate the fun from zero to ten, with zero meaning the worst time imaginable, and ten was a heavenly experience.

Now ask yourself what you'd have to change to raise that enjoyment rating by one point. When you are clearly up one point, repeat the question. How can I raise my rating by one more point?

Activity, for it to be of benefit to you, must be fun. It is often the case that when we were young, we were traumatized by being picked last in elementary school games. Then we were further damaged by the vicious pleasure the athletic children took at hitting us with the dodge ball first. So

27

it wouldn't be surprising to find that many people who would benefit from physical activity avoid it.

But activity can and should be fun. Reflect on how toddlers are naturally active and energetic. They run, they jump, they roll around. They positively adore playing games, catching and throwing, and revel in their physical bodies. All we are really doing is getting back to our true, natural selves when we embrace a more physically active life. It isn't hard, but it does sometimes take some persistence and thought. How can we make it fun?

What have we covered?

● Movement is good therapy for lifting our moods. Stay active by:

- Walks with friends.
- Moderate but challenging goals.
- Low-key team sports.
- Making it fun.

TRY THIS: Keep a diary of your moods, rating from 0 (worst) to 10 (best mood ever) each day. For a week, incorporate physical activity each day, and see if your mood lifts.

Fears and Anxieties:

Advantages of Living a Fear Free Life.

Chapter 4
Changing Our Thinking

"If you realized how powerful your thoughts are, you would never think a negative thought."
– Peace Pilgrim

Imagine you have a horse-drawn carriage. You own two horses, but you can only put reins onto one horse. So guiding your carriage will be more difficult because you can turn one horse (the one on the left) and you cannot turn the one on the right. Fortunately, if you do turn the one on the left, the horse on the right will eventually follow.

You have two sides to your brain, the right, emotional side, and the left, logical side. On the left side is language. On the right side is global and impressionistic thinking. On the left side is analysis, on the right side are pictures of how the world fits together. The right front is active when you are worried, fearful, anxious. The left side is more active when you are experiencing happy or confident feelings.

You cannot directly change your feelings, your emotional reactions, but you can change the thoughts (the left side). And when we change our thoughts, our feelings will eventually follow.

Some therapists have jumped to the conclusion that this fact means that all feelings are caused by our thoughts. If we think or say to ourselves, "Oh, an angry bear," then we feel frightened. It was supposed that the thought caused the feeling. This turned out to not be true at all. Our thoughts do not cause all of our feelings. Sometimes the feeling occurs first and our thoughts follow it. Our brain has the capacity to react with feeling and action without conscious thought. We have instinctive reactions that can save our lives before our conscious mind knows what is happening.

> *Innate, natural fears are pain, heights, and loud noises. Even those can be mastered. All other fears are learned, and can be easily un-learned.*
> – Lynn Johnson

Regardless, our thoughts are easier to change than our feelings. The carriage has two horses, and we can only guide one. While our emotions seem to just occur, we can direct our thoughts. So if anxiety or worry are getting in the way of your happiness, you deserve a chapter on how to change your thoughts.

There are many techniques for this, and people have written entire books on the subject. I am only going to do a single chapter, and I will only emphasize one technique. It may or may not be right for you. If you research "cognitive therapy" or "cognitive-behavioral therapy" you will find many resources, most of them excellent. I will end this chapter with another very useful technique, if you don't like the one I emphasize. There are always more ways to accomplish a goal.

A Favorite Technique

A wise Greek philosopher once said, "I have noticed that people are not disturbed so much by things as by their opinions about those things." (Epictetus) This means that what bothers us is really our own habitual ways of thinking, not what actually happens to us. Our opinions, or our own thoughts sometimes stop being our servants and become our masters. The job of thinking is to make us capable and confident. When our thoughts make us feel miserable, it is time to put those thoughts in their place.

When you find you feel miserable for long periods of time, it is a certain sign your thoughts are no longer serving you. They have taken on a life of their own. Misery is a signal to change something. Listen to the signal.

Misery can include **anger, jealousy, fear, grief** and other unpleasant feelings. We are emphasizing fear and nervousness in this section, but the principles apply across many areas. All of these feelings are normal and natural, *when they last a short time.* Children experience bad feelings but naturally drop negative thoughts and recover quickly. They know something we have forgotten. Thoughts are supposed to be temporary. If they last a long time, then the feeling is being produced by thoughts that run through your mind over and over. This kind of thinking is called **rumination**. If you ruminate on a memory about a bad event or thought or experience, you will continue to feel the same bad feeling.

"But," you might ask, "how do I stop *ruminating* about an event or memory? Are you telling me to stop thinking about it?"

Oddly enough, if you try to make yourself stop thinking about

> *All that is human must retrograde if it does not advance.*
> – Edward Gibbon

something (like, telling yourself, "Stop thinking about that!") the attention you give the thought when trying to stop it actually empowers that thought. It comes back and persists. Thoughts survive and grow when we give them energy and attention. Being upset at a thought gives that thought energy and attention. Naturally, it doesn't go away.

Instead, we detach from the thought. We look at it with *impartiality*. Maybe it is just a negative thought and doesn't really mean anything. We lose interest when we see something as useless or irrelevant. When we lose interest in something, it stops occurring to us. We teach ourselves that the thought is not useful or important, and it gradually withers away. If you lose interest in upsetting thoughts they will wither away.

Detaching from fear thoughts seems counter-intuitive. After all, when something frightens us, our thoughts are naturally drawn to that. Like a wreck on the freeway, we can barely shift our attention away from our fears. Unfortunately, that kind of obsessing about our worries or fears only works well in a primitive environment where our instinct serves us well. If a wolf threatens our sheep, our instinct is to drive it away. We don't need higher level thinking.

But most of the time, fear actually hurts us. When we are fearful, the highest brain levels, the frontal lobes, shift to the sidelines. Frontal lobes help us plan and decide, invent and develop, and they turn off when fear controls. The primitive part of the brain is dominant. So our brain actually plays a dirty trick on us. We need to be calm and thoughtful to deal with modern threats but instead our instincts want to run the show.

This is why it isn't useful to think about the worry or fear. It just makes our thinking sluggish and ineffective. Once we set aside our fears, new insights come from our frontal lobes and we handle the feared situation much better than we ever could have, had we remained fearful.

Try this process for a month or two. All it requires is a bit of awareness. You will be solving your problems in a calm and confident way. If you don't find that you are smarter when you are calm, you can always go back to being worried and fearful.

Step 1 DECISION:

Analyze the thought in a completely new way. Most people want to decide whether the thought is true or false. This is not the point. Thoughts are only *helpful* or *unhelpful*. You need to look at the pros and cons of thinking that thought. Does it help you? Does it give you a clear head? A peaceful heart? Does it help you feel confident and calm and relaxed? After all, we all know we function at our best when we feel good, do we not?

Are you ready to feel better? Are you ready to see that peace is more important than 'being right' no matter how upset we are? Commit yourself to supporting thoughts that support a peaceful heart.

Step 2 ACTION:

If you decide you are ruminating on a thought, that it is not helpful, and you would be better off personally if you could drop that thought, then begin the detachment process:

A. *SELF-AWARENESS*: Notice when you are feeling the negative emotion most strongly. Track down the thought that is giving you that feeling. Identify the thought. It is usually a thought about yourself or someone else that is judgmental and negative.

B. *INSIGHT*: Realize the thought gives you the bad feeling. Become aware that it is not the situation that is now affecting you, it is just the thought that is in your head. The thought is not serving you. It is controlling you. *This point is very important. You need to recognize it is not the situation that causes you to feel bad, it is your own thinking.*

C. *DETACHMENT*: Now comment on the thought: "That thought is not helpful. I don't have to think it. It is not useful. I am not obligated to pay attention to it." When the thought bounces back, just *gently* tell yourself, "I find that thought useless. I don't have to pay attention to it." (If you are upset or angry with yourself for thinking the thought, it will just give the thought more energy and it will come back more and more. It is important to be gentle and respectful to yourself.)

Recognize: "That thought doesn't mean what I think it means." That is, the thought seems to mean you should pay attention to it. Actually, you do not have to pay attention at all! It is just a bad habit of ruminating on things that aren't really important. Focus on that truth. "That thought just comes from a bad habit in my brain, and it doesn't really mean anything."

D. *REFOCUS*: Do something positive and pleasant. Reward yourself for dealing with that thought. Keep a list of small positive things you can do that will raise your spirits, such as a walk with a dog, work in the garden, and so on.

E. *PATIENCE & APPRECIATION*: Eventually the thought will fade, and you will feel more peaceful. Now appreciate that feeling. It is important to show some gratitude and appreciation for good feelings. Pay attention to good feelings, and just notice briefly when you have bad feelings. Never analyze bad feelings because that just gives them more power.

Step 3 MAINTAIN YOUR GAINS:

Whenever the thought reoccurs you will notice it has less and less emotional impact on you. Giving sincere appreciation to yourself helps. Your mind is detoxifying the thought, without you even having to know about it. Take some pleasure and satisfaction in noticing how your mind heals old wounds when you stop ruminating. Your biggest danger is in tolerating emotional pain when actually you would be better off to detach from that pain. There is very little to be gained from feeling bad.

Our minds are made to function with curiosity, openness, constant learning, and even love and joy. When those are present, we are in a state of highest functioning. We solve problems not with anxiety and anger, but with insight and creativity. We do things for the sheer joy of it. Our ordinary tasks seem interesting, just as when

> *Our minds are made to function with curiosity, openness, constant learning, and even love and joy. When those are present, we are in a state of highest functioning.*

we were innocent children, when each task, from washing dishes to watching ants, seemed endlessly entertaining. When we are at peace, we rediscover that deep inner state of perfect mental health. It is always there, just waiting for our negative thoughts to quiet down and get out of the way.

The ABCDE Technique

As I said, feelings are not necessarily caused by thought. The opposite may be true. Feelings often actually occur about a quarter to a half second before our thoughts. But we have learned that we can eventually change our feelings, our emotions, when we change our habitual ways of thinking. By challenging our own beliefs, we eventually notice our emotions are less negative. We begin to feel more accepting. The goal is to develop beliefs that support neutral or positive feelings.

In order to change thoughts, we need to write down honestly what we are thinking. Use the A-B-C-D-E format. When you become aware that you are feeling down or angry or blue or frightened, take a minute and write down the following.

- Adverse event:
- Belief:
- Consequent feeling:
- Dispute the Belief:
- Effect of disputing the belief:

Keep this up for several weeks. Actually write down these steps. Just thinking abut them doesn't have the needed change power. It takes time for the beliefs to work backwards into influencing our emotions and feelings. Follow this format:

A: What was the Adverse event? What triggered a feeling of nervousness or fear in you? Was it something you didn't want to face?

B: What is your Belief about that event? What do you think it means? What is the worst thing that you think might happen? It isn't helpful to try to analyze whether the belief is true or false, just notice what the belief is.

C: What is the Consequent feeling? What do you feel because of your belief? Again, we aren't analyzing the feeling, just noticing it.

D: How can you Dispute that belief? What evidence is there that your belief is too narrow, or wrong, or overlooking important aspects?

E: What is the Effect of disputing that Belief? How do you feel now? Here is a good point to analyze. It is always helpful to analyze our successes.

Watch carefully for times when you are definitely feeling an unpleasant emotional reaction. Then write down and describe the event ('A'). Think about what you think that event means , the 'B' or belief. List your 'C' or emotional consequence of the belief.

What about challenging the Belief? Well, usually we overlook exceptions. We say "That means I am no good as a mother" when actually there are many things you do as a mother that are good! Think of some exceptions that would bring into question the Belief.

We might think of logical flaws in the belief. If you can think of something like that, please write it down. Perhaps you are thinking in black-and-white terms, what we call all-or-nothing thinking. When you find an exception to the rule, challenge the thought with that.

Another logical flaw is "catastrophic thinking." That means we imagine something happening and say to ourselves something along the lines of "That would be awful." A good counter to that is to be a bit tough-minded, and say, "No, it wouldn't be awful, just inconvenient." Therapist Albert Ellis once cured himself of a fear of flying by saying, "Well, if the plan crashes and I die, that wouldn't be awful, since I will die sooner or later. It would just be an inconvenience." He didn't feel like it was an inconvenience, he felt it would be a catastrophe. But he stubbornly kept saying, "it would just be inconvenient, if my life were suddenly over" and after a couple of months he got on a plane with comfort. The plane was flying through turbulence and he found himself annoyed – but not frightened – that he couldn't get much work done because of how the plane was bouncing around.

Neutrality About Fear Signals

I encourage you to desensitize yourself to the actual fear triggers. There are feeling states, like a pounding heart or a tightness in the throat, or butterflies in the stomach. These tell you that you are fearful. But they are tricky. When you feel those signals, you become more fearful. You are in a vicious circle. The fear signals make you more fearful.

Make a list of the physical signs of fear. Each person is different, and your triggers are not the same as other people's triggers. Analyze which your signs are. These are triggers, so when you start to get nervous, and you feel a trigger, it reinforces your nervousness and anxiety. You become fearful of your own feeling, allergic to your own sign of anxiety.

Desensitize yourself. Imagine you are feeling that fear sign, and develop a *neutrality* about that. For example, if a pounding heart tells you "this is dangerous," and makes you more nervous, then the pounding of the heart itself increases your worry and nervousness.

Using your ABCDE format, retrain your thoughts about that feeling. For example:

A: "My skin is flushed and my fingers tingle" (an Adverse Event, since those feelings cause you to feel even more frightened.)

B: "I believe that I am going to lose control or go crazy." (You interpret those feelings as a sign of terrible danger.)

C: "That makes me even more frightened and anxious."

D: "Those feelings of flushing and tingling are just a sign that something scared me. They really don't mean what I think they mean. They just mean I over-reacted to something. It is no big deal. My body over-reacted. It is not a horrible event, just an unpleasant physical reaction. That is something I can easily tolerate. I don't have to change those feelings, I can just notice them and let them pass."

E: What effect does it have on the feelings when you Dispute them? Generally people find that when they accept the feelings as simply unpleasant experiences that don't need to be changed in any way, the feelings themselves diminish. It is as if our objection to the feeling of nervousness is what keeps it going, and when we accept it, paradoxically it leaves.

Change the Thoughts, Change the World

There is a great deal of truth to the idea that when our thoughts change, our world changes. Epictetus learned and taught that two thousand years ago, and it is still true. Watch your thoughts. So many people believe that they need to take their thoughts so very seriously. Why should we?

> *"In the beginner's mind are many possibilities; in the expert's mind, few. Strive, therefore to have a beginner's mind."*
> – Zen Buddhist saying.

What have we covered?

● Our thoughts are supposed to serve us, but we may find we are slaves to our thoughts. We can chose our thoughts based on the effect they have on us.

• Helpful thoughts give us peace, courage, and openness.

• We don't have to fight unhelpful thoughts, just dismiss them. They don't help. Drop them.

• Appreciating helpful thoughts will energize them.

• The ABCDE technique can also desensitize our unhelpful thoughts.

Try this: Note in your diary how people are caught up in their own thinking and fail to see the possibilities all around them. Then ask yourself what you might be overlooking because of how your own thinking habits put blinders on you.

Chapter 5
Training Our Brains

"Nobody can go back and start a new beginning, but anyone can start today and make a new ending."
– Maria Robinson

A dog is barking in the night.

"Raouff, raouff, rauoff . . . raouff, raouff, raouff . . . raouff, raouff, raouff . . ."

You have been trying to get to sleep. The dog's bark penetrates your brain, through the pillow clenched tightly around your head. "If only that stupid dog would stop it," you think to yourself. You feel angry, so angry, you wish you could shut the dog up.

There are only two categories of things to worry about: things you can control, and things you cannot control.

If you can't control something, there is no point in worrying about it, so you might as well accept it.

If you can control something, there is no point in worrying about it, you might as well go ahead and do something about it.

Doing Something About It

What would you do? You might put in ear plugs and try to ignore the dog, and this might work. Often it doesn't because as you try to ignore that barking dog, it still seeps through into your brain. It irritates all the more, because your efforts to shut out the sound are defeated.

What if I can show you a way to deal with that dog? How would that be a blessing to you? Perhaps you don't have noisy dogs in your neighborhood, so you aren't very interested. Well, what about things that do irritate you? What about a snoring spouse, an obnoxious boss, an irritating neighbor . . . what about an hyperactive child? There are so many times in life that we are faced with unpleasant things we cannot change, but things we find noxious. How do we deal with them?

My Discovery

Something like that happened to me one night, and I used a simple tool that I had shared with many patients over the years. I want to share it with you.

It wasn't a dog, it was a group of teenagers. They had some firecrackers, and one evening as I was drifting off to sleep, I heard "bang-bang-bang-bang-bang . . ." as they set off a string. It startled me and I woke up. I got comfortable, but about ten minutes later, as I was drifting off again, here came that same noise, the machine-gun reports of another string. I recognized the reality of the situation. They were drifting around the neighborhood, setting off their prize firecrackers from time to time, and there was really nothing I could do about it.

Then I realized that was not true. For the next ten minutes, I systematically changed something about my own brain, and the next time a string of crackers reverberated through my little neighborhood, I was ready, and as I heard them, I went right off to sleep! Believe it or not, my brain reacted in such a way as to put me right into a satisfying sleep state before that string had played itself out!

I want to help you learn the tool I used. It is fairly simple, taking about ten minutes. If you practice it once a day, for ten minutes each time, you will have something to help you deal with all kinds of irritations and difficulties.

The tool I used is called "Autogenic Training." It was developed to help people program their minds and bodies in health-producing ways. I have found that almost everyone can learn this tool, if they are willing to practice. I encourage you to try it right now.

Hope is both the earliest and the most indispensable virtue inherent in the state of being alive. If life is to be sustained hope must remain, even where confidence is wounded, trust impaired.
– Erik H. Erikson

Self Hypnosis for Dummies

These autogenic training exercises can help you recover from anxiety, stress, and tension. These exercises have also been shown to aid in the recovery from certain diseases in which stress plays a part, such as headaches, high blood pressure, some stomach and bowel problems, and so on. Those who practice this skill every day sleep better and keep their blood pressure lower.

How do we practice? Proceeding through the phrases below, repeat every phrase, silently, in your mind, *three times*. Say the phrase in a quiet, thoughtful way. Focus all your attention on that part of the body being mentioned. For example, when you say, "My right arm feels heavy," then focus your attention on the feelings in the right arm. Pause after and notice how you feel. Focus on your feelings for two or three breaths. Practice each set of exercises until you are quite automatic with them.

Practice at least once, better, twice a day. I believe the best time is in the middle of the day, around lunch. The more often you return your body to a state of restful quiet, the more energy and self-control you will experience. One patient of mine had irritable bowel syndrome, a painful and dangerous illness. She stopped her symptoms entirely by practicing five times a day. I was amazed and asked, "How did you do that?" She said that before going to work, she practiced for about ten minutes. At work they had a mid-morning break, and she practiced again for ten minutes. At lunch she'd excuse herself from her friends and practice again. Afternoon break? Autogenic training time. And when she came home from work, she went through about fifteen minutes of practice. Her gut pain, her constipation and diarrhea had stopped. For her, five practices a day was a small price to pay.

Set 1: (Remember to pause and notice how you feel after each phrase)

I feel quite quiet. . . I am easily relaxed. . . . My right arm feels heavy . . . My left arm feels heavy . . . My arms feel heavy and relaxed . . . My right leg feels heavy. . . My left leg feels heavy . . . My arms and legs feel heavy and relaxed . . . My hips and stomach are quiet and relaxed . . . My breathing is calm and regular . . . My heartbeat is calm and regular . . . My shoulders are heavy . . . My face is smooth and quiet . . .I am beginning to feel quite relaxed. . .

Set 2:

My right hand is warm. . . Warmth flows into my right hand . . . My left hand is warm. . . Warmth flows into my left hand . . . Warmth flows into my hands. . . My hands are warm. . . My right foot is warm. . . My left foot is warm. . . My hands and feet are warm. . . Warmth flows into my hands and feet . . . My eyes are comfortably warm and peaceful . . . My forehead is cool and my eyes are warm . . . I am warm and peaceful .

Set 3:

I am beginning to feel quite relaxed. . . My breathing is calm and regular. . . My heartbeat is calm and regular. . . I am at peace. . . Sounds and sights around contribute to peace. . . Peace goes with me throughout the day . . . There is nothing to bother and nothing to disturb. . .

Set 4:

My mind is quiet . . . My mind enjoys being quiet . . . My thoughts are calm and quiet . . . There is nothing to bother and nothing to disturb . . . My mind is quiet . . . I feel good when my mind is quiet . . .

Set 5:

Just for today, I will anger not, I will worry not . . . I will be grateful and humble . . . I will do my work with appreciation . . . I will be kind to all . . .

How did I use Autogenic Training to deal with the firecrackers? I simply created my own set of phrases and repeated them to myself. First I worked for heavy arms and legs and warm hands and feet. Once I had those sensations I knew I had succeeded at creating a quiet inner state, and that my mind would accept suggestions. After a few minutes of the following phrases, my brain had achieved a new response, and it really worked. Here are the phrases I created:

"The sound of firecrackers reminds me to relax . . . The sound of firecrackers makes me relax . . . When I hear firecrackers, I relax . . . When I hear firecrackers, I feel sleepy and peaceful . . . The sounds of firecrackers make me sleepy . . . I feel sleepy and peaceful now and when I hear firecrackers . . . I am at peace with firecrackers . . . There is peace hiding inside the sounds of firecrackers . . . Firecrackers make be sleepy . . . Firecrackers make me peaceful . . . Firecrackers are comforting to me . . ."

As I was working through those phrases, I heard another string go off. This time, instead of alerting me, it felt like someone had given me some kind of anesthetic! I recall the last thought I had just before I drifted completely off to sleep: "Ah, (slight smile) it worked." You can see why I think of Autogenic Training as "Self Hypnosis for Dummies."

The barking dog . . . that dog will continue to bark whether you are annoyed or not. Why not change the meaning of the barking in your mind?

"The barking dog drives away fears . . . The barking drives away tension . . . When I hear the barking, I remember to relax . . . When I hear the barking, I feel relaxed and peaceful . . . The sound of barking makes me feel secure and relaxed . . . I am grateful for the watchful dog . . . I feel peaceful, secure and sleepy . . ." I predict that soon you will drift off.

Being Sure I Am on the Right Track

Now just to prove to me that the firecracker experience was not a fluke, chance provided me with another opportunity to do something similar. (I wonder how often chance might be actually some hidden blessing we don't recognize at the time. Could our so-called random events be opportunities? A friend of mine likes to say, "Opportunities don't knock once, they are knocking all the time. We just don't recognize the sound.")

I had taken my family on a little family camp-out. We found a campground and set up the tent, ate supper, and crawled into our sleeping bags, thinking excitedly about the great adventures we were going to have the next day. Then I realized something. We were camped close to the road, and I became aware of large trucks whining down the road toward a small near-by town. As quiet descended on the campground, the "jake brake" truck sounds rolled across the campground. Since I am the lightest sleeper in the family, I figured I was the only one bothered by that sound.

Again, I used my Autogenic Training tool, and used these ideas:

"Trucks carry away troubles and cares . . . The trucks bring blessings and gifts . . . Each truck is carrying away all my tension and worry . . . As the trucks pass by, they carry away my tension and worry . . . There is nothing left to worry or bother . . . I am empty of tension and worry, and I feel peace . . . The sounds of trucks comfort me . . . I feel comfortable listening to the trucks . . . The trucks are kind and love to serve me . . . They carry away all troubles and cares . . . I feel at peace . . . I am at peace . . . Truck sounds make me sleepy . . . When I hear trucks I feel sleepy."

Again, my tool worked wonders for me. I fell asleep in a few minutes and slept very peacefully. I was shocked the next morning when the rest of my family complained bitterly about being kept up all night by the sounds of large trucks on the highway! I was embarrassed to realize I had misjudged the situation, assuming I was the only one awake. I should have shared what I was doing with my poor family who was suffering as I had been.

Practice Autogenic Training once a day, then use it to solve simple problems of meaning. It is a wonderful and useful way to tame the wild amygdala, that mini-brain that switches your brain's stress system on or off. What things mean is not determined in the stars, but in our own heart and mind. We get to chose meanings, although most of the time, we chose automatically. Autogenic training is simply a way to make that choice conscious. Choose to see things in a peaceful way.

Chapter 6
Confront Fear, Create Courage

*"The secret of life is this: When you hear
cannons, walk toward them."*
– Marcel France

I f nervousness and anxiety have been your problem, you should be
feeling more calm by now. The next step is to walk toward the
cannons.

Fear can only live on anxiety. My friend Bill O'Hanlon tells the story
of Vishnu and the Fear Monster. It seems that the Hindu God Vishnu had
to go on a long trip. As he left his castle, he told the other minor gods that
they should not open the castle door while he was gone.

When he returned, the door was wide open. Walking into the castle,
Vishnu saw room after room in dishevel. Scowling he walked to the very
back of the castle. There in the corner, quivering and whimpering,

cowered all the gods. Looming over them was a huge, ugly monster. Vishnu walked into the room.

"I told you guys, 'don't open the door, don't let anyone in,' and now look, the castle is a wreck. When will you ever learn to listen?"

"But . . . but . . . but . . . the monster!" they cried.

"Oh, yes, I know this one," said Vishnu. "He's the Fear Monster. He lives off fears, so when you run from him, he grows. Wasn't he about two feet tall when you let him in?"

The gods admitted that he was like a munchkin and even looked cute, so they had thought to adopt him.

"Then he did something to scare you, and when you jumped back, he grew, didn't he?"

Yes, they admitted, that is what had happened.

"Well," continued Vishnu, "the poor guy has been chasing you ever since and growing, and you have been running and feeding him your fear. Now look him right in the eye and remember how cute and small he was."

The Fear Monster began to shrink. This made them smile, and poor old FM shrank even more. Finally he was back to his real size, a cute munchkin again, and Vishnu let the gods keep him around the castle to remind them to always face fears and never run from them.

Fear Lives on Avoidance

By walking toward the sound of cannon, as Marcel France says, we put fear on a diet. Courage is simply rising above what your primitive brain is telling you and doing what needs to be done, whether you are afraid or not.

But if you have been feeding fears for years and years, your own personal Fear Monster is pretty big and ugly. A patient of mine came from a religious family and their custom was to attend a church service every Sabbath. But my patient became afraid that in Sunday School he would be asked questions and would stutter or be confused. He would look stupid. He was panicked about that, and avoided church.

Each Sabbath he was feeding his Fear Monster a large helping of high energy food. By staying home, his courage was starving. How can he put Fear on a diet?

I suggested he simply go to church and stay only until his fear began to diminish. As soon as he felt the fear starting to shrink, he could reward himself by going home again. The idea is that you shrink fear by forcing it to face courage. As soon as it diminishes you have won the contest. You have made the Fear Bully back down.

Imaginary Fears

Some fears are not of places and things, but of future worries. In this case, I would say your problem is that you are not worrying enough. Worrisome persons usually have vague worries that they try to not think about. They aren't working hard enough at worry.

Schedule your worries. Set aside an hour per day when you will do nothing but worry. Then face each possible worry. Instead of trying to make it less, make it more vivid and scary. Keep focusing on that vivid and scary image until you feel your breathing begin to slow and your heart begin to calm.

As you think of each worry or fear, blow it up to enormous proportions. Now imagine how you would survive. It may help to think to yourself, "That is not horrible, just inconvenient."

> *"Courage is not simply one of the virtues, but the form of every virtue at the testing point."*
> – C. S. Lewis

One woman was fearful that if she left her house, her parents would die. By vividly experiencing that imaginary catastrophe, she realized that her fear was totally true. One day, her parents would die. She may still be alive, and they would be dead. After all, the number of people who either have died or will die is 100%, is it not? Now she imagined preparing their funeral.

"What if I freeze and can't speak at the funeral?" she worried. She imagined all the people criticizing and condemning her for failing to honor her parents. Walk toward the cannons. Usually she would think of a frightening scene and then try to stop thinking of it. She imagined the worst possible outcome and froze up.

She didn't stop thinking this time. She kept the funeral scene in mind until she began to see it as simply an uncomfortable, unpleasant experience. (That usually takes about a half hour.) I suggested to her that it is really none of her business what other people think about her, anyway, so she should contemplate their judgment with neutrality. She did that, and her fear began to subside.

Her homework was to imagine death, judgment and condemnation every day for an hour until she felt genuinely neutral about those situations.

When we don't run, fear itself must run from us.

Our Feelings Betray Us

Some people have panic attacks. They have become fearful of their own feelings. As we suggested in the last chapter, their own fear makes them fearful.

Most panic attacks set in when people start to feel uncomfortable. They might feel short of breath or they feel their heart pound. Perhaps their fingers tingle. Or they feel dizzy or even nausea. Such feelings remind them of awful panic from the past and they are terrified they will have that same feeling again.

But what if they walked toward the cannons? What if they courted, so to speak, the very feeling they fear? The best way to desensitize ourselves is to do the very thing we fear. If you are afraid of your own inner feelings, you can brainstorm ways to make those feelings happen. Within thirty minutes of practicing the feared feeling, you will already find you are far more immune.

A person who is short of breath can breathe through a straw for a minute or two. A person who fears the pounding of the heart can run up and down stairs for a few minutes and then study that pounding feeling. A person who is afraid of dizziness can spin around for a minute or two. As you feel the particular feeling that you have feared, use the principle of

Autogenic Training: Tell yourself that the feeling doesn't mean what you think it means, and that it is perfectly safe.

So if you are persecuted by panic, become the panic's persecutor. Try to make those feelings happen and keep them happening for thirty minutes or so. After a while, that feeling of fear is simply an inconvenient and unpleasant experience. Tell yourself that an unpleasant feeling, even a strong one, cannot harm you. It is just an unpleasant feeling. It doesn't really mean anything.

What have we covered?

● We overcome anxieties by walking toward them.

• Schedule worry times and blow the worry up to ridiculous proportions.

• Do the thing you fear.

• Panic attacks are caused by fear of our own feelings. Practice bringing the sensations you fear into your life for thirty minutes at a time.

● Fear-free and worry free life is possible and desirable. Your fears are unnecessary burdens you have acquired. Drop them and live a more joyful life.

Try this: Interview friends who seem to be more fearless. Ask them how it helps their lives to be confident and zestful.

Resolving Anger

Ways of Overcoming Anger and Reasons Why You Should.

Chapter 7
Why Anger Doesn't Work . . . and What to Do About It

"Holding on to anger is like grasping a hot coal with the intent of throwing it at someone else; you are the one who gets burned."
– Buddha

Perhaps anger is a practical joke that Mother Nature has played on the human race. In a primitive society, anger helps us survive. We can fight off aggressors or drive away bears or lions from our flocks with the energy that anger gives us. But in a civilized society, anger generally backfires and causes much trouble.

The reason for this is very simple: When we are angry we are less intelligent. The part of our brain that directs anger is called the "reptile brain." It gives us the energy to fight our enemies. We react primitively and instinctively. The higher brain is quiet, on the sidelines. We lose our ability to think clearly and intelligently. And in a modern society, thinking clearly is vital. While anger helped our ancestors survive, today it makes it very hard for us to flourish. We *can* challenge anger. We *can* set our goal to be more calm, intelligent, and effective. We *can* decide to not let anger control us.

Reflect on the Usefulness of Anger

Recognize that while anger is a natural part of ourselves, it is also generally not helpful. If you wish to live a more calm, intelligent, and effective life, start here. Think thoughtfully and deeply about how effective anger is in your life. How is it working so far?

You can see from reflecting on it that when we use anger we generally get nowhere. We might yell and storm at family members and they temporarily change. But soon they go right back to doing what they did before. So we yell and storm some more, which temporarily helps. But when you look at the whole picture, you see that being chronically angry does nothing to help create better situations. It just drives the problems underground. And they do pop up again, don't they?

"Anger dwells only in the bosom of fools."
– Albert Einstein

What about anger with people outside of the family, such as those who drive in irresponsible ways? Aren't you justified in becoming angry with those people? After all, aren't they a menace to safe driving? Actually if you take a broad view, you will see that challenging a dangerous driver is just creating more danger. As we said, people are less intelligent when angry. They do irrational things. They act impulsively. Do you really want the bad driver in the other car acting even more irrationally and impulsively? Well, that is what you get when you try to correct their behavior. They get angry and therefore they are dumb and don't learn from your anger.

So getting angry with people in traffic is actually a problem of excessive optimism on your part. You really believe it will help them to be mad at them, but when you take a broader view, you can see that the anger didn't work.

What Is the Real Result of Anger?

Our challenge is to look at whether anger really helps. The comic Richard Pryor once set himself on fire while using drugs. He later said, "I jumped up, and I was on fire! And I ran out of the house on fire! And I ran down the street on fire! And I learned something from that. I learned that when you are on fire, running down the street, *people get out of your way!*"

> *"How much more grievous are the consequences of anger than the causes of it."*
> – Marcus Aurelius

Could looking at anger like that help you? Do you see an advantage to recognizing that all anger does is to get people to jump back away from you, but it doesn't really help? It doesn't really change anything for the better? People you don't know generally learn nothing of value from your anger. People you are close to simply learn that they need to be fearful of you. Since fear and love cannot exist in the same person at the same time, anger is robbing you of the love that we all want and need.

What Causes Anger?

"He really made me mad!" The most common way we have of understanding anger is that it is a reaction to what happens to us. As we watch people deal with emotions, it does seem likely that events and people do make us mad. Something happens and then there is an angry response.

There is some truth to that understanding. After all, you are likely to become angry with someone on the road who honks aggressively or who flashes rude hand gestures. In our own families, we are more likely to be angry when others contradict us or argue with us or discount us. But that is just a surface analysis. Let's look deeper.

How Our Thinking Controls us

Actually, it is a combination of what happens to us and what kinds of thoughts we habitually entertain in our minds that causes anger. A quick mental experiment proves that this is true.

Imagine five men, all the same age, all with the same general background. In each case, a rude driver cuts each man off, honks aggressively, and makes the exact same rude gesture. Does each man become equally angry? Of course not. It is immediately obvious that each man will react differently. One is furious, one is annoyed, one is amused by the immaturity shown, one feels guilty, and one didn't even notice. What accounts for the difference? It lies in the *habits of thinking* of each person.

One man has a habit of thinking more peacefully, and he thinks that people who are rude in traffic are silly and short-sighted. So he feels sorry for someone so silly as to act that way. Another man is in the habit of thinking that the world is full of rotten, no-good people who need to be put in their place. Does it surprise us to see that the second man becomes quite angry?

A Better View

I invite you to view the problem of anger as one of our own habit, not something that others cause us to feel. This is a better view because it means there is something that we can do about anger. If anger were caused by other people, there would be no hope. We would go through our life reacting as we always have, and we couldn't change.

My view is that we are ultimately responsible for how we feel. Sometimes clients resist this view because they are secretly fearful of "being to blame" for the anger. That is understandable. Many people grow up in families where "who is to blame" is an important question. The theory seems to be that if we can find out who is to blame and punish him, everything will be better.

This childhood fear of being blamed is groundless. We innocently drift into bad habits, so blame is silly. But we can be accountable. When we take responsibility for our own feelings, we begin to feel more free and flexible. We are no longer slaves to what happens to us. The world brims with possibilities.

Is Anger Ever Positive?

We do sometimes see people who have suppressed anger, who have kept it inside and never spoken up about what they want. They were never peaceful and insightful, and they were also never obviously angry. Instead they kept it bottled up inside. They tell us that getting "in touch with anger" was a helpful experience for them. It gave them the energy to get up and do what needed to be done. So there are times when anger produces a good outcome. For those people, acknowledging anger is an important positive step. It isn't the end of the journey, just a first step.

The problem is that *most often*, the use of anger to get our way is not helpful. It makes other people angry, so we end up with a world full of angry people. When we get our way because of our anger, we haven't really earned the changes. Other people are not cooperating with us, and they are clearly not changing what they do out of enlightened self interest or from love and respect for us. Instead, they do it because they are afraid of our anger. We run at them on fire, and all they do is jump out of our way.

So anger is a way to have an impact, but it is cheating, a form of emotional blackmail. Instead of earning respect and mutual cooperation, we force others to bend to our will. That will always have a high price.

Fear of Giving up Anger

Sometimes we are actually afraid to give up something even when it doesn't work. We don't know what we will replace it with. That is a reasonable fear. We should be cautious about giving up something that we know.

Reflecting on the problem you will see that some people do not get angry and their lives work well. Perhaps you can develop some curiosity about how they do that, and how you could learn more of how to do that?

What Is Behind Anger?

Insecurity: First, most often there is a feeling of *insecurity*. When we feel fearful, out of control, or threatened, we might respond with anger. Clearly the feeling of insecurity is not one we tolerate well. Insecurity seems to say to us, "I am NOT OKAY." What an unwelcome feeling! We don't seem to be able to admit we have such a feeling. Instead we flee to a feeling where we feel more in control, that of indignation or resentment or even rage. In all of those we feel more of a "I am okay, and you are not okay."

So you can see this type of anger – the most common kind – as a *defense*, something that allows us to manage uncomfortable emotions.

If you write in your diary about the things that make you angry, you may discover that is the case. Just before the anger, there may have been a moment of insecurity, and you fled that feeling and resorted to anger. Just becoming aware of that allows us a more powerful option, namely one of vulnerability.

This may seem ridiculous. After all, what is to be gained by focusing your attention on the insecure feeling instead of being angry?

The answer is that when we acknowledge our real feeling of insecurity, people tend to be more understanding and accepting. They might listen better. They may be able to have some empathy for us. This starts us on a path toward negotiating a reasonable agreement. It is much better than anger.

Control: Some people enjoy controlling others, not out of insecurity but paradoxically out of too much security. These folks feel entitled to dominate and control. They have self esteem that is too high, not too low. Their self-esteem is unrealistic. They think they can do no wrong.

These people, the control addicts, can be very dangerous people. They take pleasure from anger, and from causing pain. When they get angry, their heart rate slows down, and they get icy calm. They might do anything in order to boss and control. They can be brutal.

We don't have good treatment for these people. They generally cannot be helped. I hope you are not one of them.

How Anger Keeps Going; How We Can Derail Anger

Anger is a reaction to a threatening situation. It is related to the *fight or flight* response in the brain, automatic and instinctive reactions to stress. When we get angry, we have decided (at an instinctive level) that we do not have to run away, we can probably win the fight. The anger gives us the energy to harm or even kill our opponent.

In our civilized society, hurting and killing are very serious affairs, and there is far too much of it. So as we become angry, it is vital that we pause. The best thing to do when we are angry is hold back. Don't say anything, don't do anything. It may be that our anger is because of our own insecurities. Perhaps we are fearful or uncertain and we "solve" that feeling with our anger. But that solution skips over the insecurity. It perpetuates the insecurity, because instead of actually working on overcoming the insecurity, we turn the problem outwards.

But if we pause and think about the need to understand our own reaction, the initial anger may be replaced by a more thoughtful and intelligent assessment. Stop, think about what you really want. Don't show anger, but rather think about what is in your best interest. You will likely find that this is actually a very difficult step, because you are opposing your brain's instincts. You will notice that you have a tendency to replay the situation over and over in your mind. You recall the insult or problem and think on it repeatedly. You ruminate. Your mind gets stuck on this memory and runs it over and over. Of course, as long as you ruminate, you continue to be angry. If you ruminate on a memory about a bad event or thought or experience, you will continue to feel the same bad feeling.

It can genuinely help to simply recall that being angry turns off the highest and best part of your brain, the frontal lobes. Why lose all that mental horsepower? Why give up your best thinking abilities just because you are angry.

I had a karate instructor once who would say to us, "You lose your temper, you lose the fight." Why lose in life? Keep your temper, keep your mind, lose your temper, lose your mind!

Immunity to Anger: An Achievable Dream

When we are young, we get vaccinations and inoculation against a variety of illnesses. Then we don't have to fear polio or typhoid. Our bodies are immune. Can we do the same thing with anger?

"The more anger towards the past you carry in your heart, the less capable you are of loving in the present."
– Barbara DeAngelis

Yes we can. And when we become less susceptible to anger, we are free to develop better ways of dealing with problems and difficulties. There is a simple three-step process that will give you your own immunity to anger. A child who receives desensitization shots to an allergy is able to feel comfortable and free to do things that he couldn't do before. Like that child, you will increase your comfort and freedom when outside forces can not disturb your own peace of mind.

Step One: **What is the opposite of anger and temper?** Most people agree that the opposite is when they feel a peaceful and calm feeling. Everyone has moments when he or she feels that. Notice when you are most peaceful and calm. Practice feeling calm. Develop an ability to be calm and peaceful. That's what this book is about, returning to your natural calm and peace.

Step Two: **Desensitize yourself to the "triggers" in our environment.** You already know how to desensitize yourself to fear triggers. Anger is the same. You can probably think of certain events that trigger your anger. Perhaps it is someone driving in a stupid and reckless fashion, or someone following you too closely. Or maybe it is events in the family.

Write down each thing that you can think of that irritates or enrages you. Estimate how much each item on your list bothers you. Put a number by each item, where 0 = no bother at all, and 10 = the most maddening thing you can think of. Be sure to write down the *very first sign* that something is about to make you angry.

Now when you practice quieting yourself, also begin to practice picturing the events on the list. Each time you think of the upsetting situation, breath deeply and slowly and concentrate on relaxing your muscles. Keep that up until you have a relaxed and calm reaction even while picturing the upsetting situation. With practice, even when the same event happens ("My spouse yells angrily at me"), you will find now that the experience just doesn't have the power to disturb you! You have achieved control over that situation! It can no longer control you, and you are more free.

Step Three: **Reframing: Find a better way to look at it.** Now that you have controlled the trigger, look deeper. When something triggers your anger, you have an assumption about the *meaning* of that behavior. If a rude driver upsets you, what do you believe about that driver? That he deserves to be taught a lesson? If a family member upsets you, what do you believe about that? Perhaps that she is not showing respect? *Write down the beliefs you have when you find anger is controlling you.*

What could another explanation be? Try to take a broader view. Look for a more peaceful way to view the situation. Maybe the person in traffic has to rush because he just heard of an emergency? Maybe your family member is not thinking clearly or is distracted?

Look at the situation again. Practice compassion and understanding. Can you see a more soothing way to look at it?

• Could there be a *positive intention* even if the behavior is bad?

"He's just trying to be playful and friendly." "She is trying to reduce her own discomfort."

• Could there be a *hidden benefit* that comes from the situation?

"This is an opportunity for me to learn patience."

• Are there *compensating factors*?

"She is generally much more positive, she must just be in a bad mood."

• Will it *soon pass* and is therefore not an important issue?

"Our finances are generally bad at this time of year, but in three months we will be fine."

If you discover a better way to view the trigger, a way that allows you to feel more compassion about the person who makes you angry, then you will be immune to anger in that situation. Keep focusing on finding a broader view, and soon you will find that you feel generally more peaceful and relaxed. You will find your thinking is clearer and people around you will feel more relaxed and at ease.

What have we covered?

● Anger shuts down the higher brain and makes us less intelligent.

● Anger is caused both by what happens to us and how we habitually think.

● We overcome anger by:
  • Practicing peace and calm,
  • Desensitizing ourselves to anger triggers, and
  • Reframing the anger triggers as opportunities or blessings in disguise.

Try this: Watch curiously when people get angry. Note things they do when they are angry that will actually end up hurting or defeating them in the long run. Note the difference between movies (where anger is glorified) and real life.

Chapter 8
Compassion and Forgiveness

The remarkable thing is that we really love our neighbor as ourselves: we do unto others as we do unto ourselves. We hate others when we hate ourselves. We are tolerant toward others when we tolerate ourselves. We forgive others when we forgive ourselves.
— Eric Hoffer

The Dalai Lama tells a story about one of his teachers who was captured by the Chinese Communist army when China invaded his country of Tibet in 1950. This teacher was held for many years in Chinese prisons and concentration camps. Finally he was released, and the Dalai Lama was eager to see his old friend. He found to his delight that the years of torture and isolation had not harmed this beloved teacher, and he was still the same gentle and kind and happy person as before. How had he managed to pass those terrible years without damage to his personality?

"Oh, it was quite difficult," replied the old monk. "There were many times I was afraid I would lose compassion for those who tortured me."

Our natural response to someone injuring us is to be angry. It is built in. But it is also natural to forgive. When we were children, we were naturally forgiving, so forgiveness is really like recalling our natural innocence.

I am going to propose that compassion and forgiveness are intimately related. Let's define some terms.

Compassion means two things: First, when we develop compassion, we have a greater sense of how other people feel. This is empathy. It is based on imagination. How would we feel if we were in the other person's shoes? It is also based on good observation. When we were little children and saw another child fall down, we then saw that youngster cry. We recognized the link: falling, crying. That little friend has been hurt!

The second thing it is based on is the golden rule. How would we want to be treated if we were hurt? Compassion sees suffering and wants to relieve that suffering. Compassion wants to lift others, because we would want to be lifted ourselves. Compassion wants to help.

Compassion as a Skill

A skill? Isn't compassion a gift, something that some people simply have and others don't? There is truth in that idea. Some people seem to be much more empathic than others, it comes easily to them, and we should call it a gift. But remember K. Anders Ericsson, our professor friend who claims that talent doesn't predict anything in the long run. While some are talented, only hard work predicts excellence in any field.

So why should one develop compassion? Professor Rich Davidson at the University of Wisconsin at Madison has found a couple of things about happiness and compassion.

First, the most compassionate are also the most happy. When students are asked to develop compassion they also raise the energy level in the left frontal lobes. That means they experience greater happiness. The higher the energy left in the left frontal area, the higher the level of happiness. So the exercise of compassion does increase happiness.

Second, compassion can be trained into the brain. In their book *Visions of Compassion,* Davidson and co-author Anne Harrington describe the steps toward higher compassion and happiness. They show that happiness is a skill like any other skill.

So how does a person develop this skill? Davidson shows that Buddhist meditation seems particularly effective. Holding attention on a single object is the key. Students are taught first to simply focus on the breathing. Observe the in-breath and the out-breath. Having achieved some skill at keeping focus on one thing, like breathing, one then uses this skill to think about the meaning of compassion. You simply reflect on the meaning of the word "compassion" and what it means to you. How does it show up in your life? What is the value of compassion? How would it be of help to you? Experience "compassion" in an ever more vivid way.

I have found that it can help to imagine that I am closely related to people whom I do not actually know. For example, imagine people moving about in a shopping center. I know none of them. What if they were long-lost brothers or sisters to me, and I didn't realize we were related? Wouldn't that soften my heart? Would I not feel some sympathy for them?

Now use that strategy in regard to some actual catastrophe. Recall the aftermath of Hurricane Katrina? Were those people suffering? Of course. No clean water, no food, no homes where those people could retreat and find comfort. If that suffering person were a close family member, you'd want to relieve their suffering.

Imagine that is happening to you. What would you want? You would want someone to relieve your suffering, wouldn't you?

What about "bad people" who commit crimes, hurt people, and take advantage of weak people? Do they deserve compassion too? After all, they are bad, are they not? Shouldn't we be angry, not compassionate to them?

Certainly it is understandable for us to feel anger when we see crimes and injustices. I believe it is deeply built into us, and even young children have a sense of justice and fairness. We are hard-wired by Mother Nature for that kind of anger. Yet sometimes what is hard-wired is not always what is best for us.

In that case, we can reflect on the concept that when people do evil things, they generally suffer for what they do. At some point, sooner or later, there is some kind of balancing out that comes, and these people do pay a price. Most religions teach this truth, that at some point there is inevitable pain that is the result of bad actions.

So we can imagine that eventual pain, and imagine the remorse and sorrow that people feel when their evil catches up with them. We can feel sad for their pain.

Or perhaps we can imagine how their life has led them to this point where they are unable to appreciate the difference between good and evil. We can think, "There but for the grace of God go I." That softens our heart.

This kind of practice can help me rise above my natural anger at those who have harmed or damaged me or my loved ones.

Imaculee Ilibagiza has written about how she survived the Rwandan holocaust in her book, *Left to Tell*. This is a true account of how she and seven other Tutsi women hid in a bathroom the size of a small closet for ninety-one days while the Hutus searched for her. They were pressed tightly together while the searchers called her name as they searched for her, vowing to kill her as they had killed other Tutsis in Rwanda.

> *If you want others to be happy, practice compassion. If you want to be happy, practice compassion.*
> – The Dalai Lama

During these harrowing times, she prayed constantly and felt a deep conviction that only a miracle from God was keeping them alive. At one point she recognized that her own anger at the Hutu butchery was making it impossible to continue to pray. As the killers searched the house, she was praying that their hiding place would be safe, and she heard the anger she felt talking to her.

"My scalp was burning," she writes, "and the ugly whispering slithered in my head again: *Why are you calling on God? Don't you have as much hatred in your heart as the killers do? Aren't you as guilty of hatred as they are? . . .How can you love God but hate so many of his creations?"*

She struggled with this anger, trying to pray yet realizing she did hate the killers and wanted them to suffer and die. She says, "It was no use–my prayers felt hollow. A war had started in my soul, and I could no longer pray to a God of love with a heart full of hatred." Finally in her prayers she admits she cannot forgive and asks to be shown how to forgive. For days she prays, scarcely taking food or water, passing the hours struggling with the idea of forgiveness for the killers.

Then one night she hears screaming near their hiding place and then a baby crying. She supposes the Hutus have killed a mother and then left the baby to die in the open. For over a day the baby cries, its cries becoming more and more feeble until finally it is silent. She asks God, *"How can I forgive people who would do such a thing to an infant?"*

She hears an answer: *"You are **all** my children . . . and the baby is with Me now."* Forgiveness comes because she sees all as children of God. Children may be cruel, thoughtless, and they may have to suffer greatly because of their mistakes, but they are children.

Later, after the killing has stopped Immaculee meets the man who slaughtered her family. The jail officer who brings this man out of his cell confronts him, yelling at him, "Look at this woman, you killed her family." Imaculee recognizes the killer. He was a Hutu from her village, a neighbor. He was man who had respect and power and now he cowers in degradation and shame. But Immaculee looks on him with compassion, brushes his trembling hands with hers, and says, "I forgive you." Tears run down their faces. The officer is angry, he wants the killer to suffer. Immaculee knows that he already suffers.

Worthington's Forgiveness Steps

These notes on forgiveness are based on work done by Dr. Everett Worthington, Jr. He suggests you think of forgiveness as being a pyramid one climbs. There are five steps to his pyramid, which you can remember by the mnemonic "REACH." I suggest you write a response to each of the five steps in your journal or diary. Write them in the form of letters. Don't go through this quickly but rather give your mind and heart time to adjust to the idea of forgiveness. Please read this section very carefully. Read it several times. Ponder and think.

R: **Recall** the pain and hurt you have suffered. True forgiveness comes when we actually have an injury to forgive, and you owe yourself the respect of acknowledging the pain. Write about it. *Write a letter* to the person who caused the pain. (You don't necessarily need to send it! That is almost never a good idea.) Describe the events and pain. Let the feelings out onto the paper.

> *"But he doesn't deserve to be forgiven!"*
> *"Honey, you don't forgive him for him. You forgive him for you."*
> – Dialog in the movie, *Diary of a Mad Black Woman*, written and directed by Tyler Perry.

Realistically look at the hurt and now let yourself wish for a relief of the pain from those feelings. Don't blame the other person, but rather just focus on your own goal of peace and forgiveness.

Sometimes I have asked people to read to me their record. They may fear sharing it. They feel as if they will break into pieces, but they will not. They will only become whole. They speak about the pain, the betrayal, the fear and anger. I listen as a witness, then we sometimes take that writing and burn it.

Research on this point is clear. People who write about the trauma do much better and recover from the trauma's effects. The more details you can put into this step, the better you will do. Unless you have been genuinely harmed, you cannot genuinely forgive. Document the harm.

> *"We are healed of a suffering only by experiencing it to the full."*
> – Marcel Proust

E: Empathize with the perpetrator of your hurt. This is a very hard step, but do-able. I have found that this step causes many people to stumble or balk. They seem to hate the idea of trying to feel empathy for an evil person. They seem to believe that they would become evil too. This is a mistake. We do not become evil when we stop judging another person, we become more fully good. If you will try this step, you will find that you feel much better.

Write about what may have motivated that person to hurt you. Try to put yourself in the shoes of that other person. *Write a letter* to yourself

84

as if you were the other person and you were trying to explain your acts. What could have motivated that person to harm you? What kinds of thoughts and beliefs might they have had? What kinds of emotions were they experiencing? Think of times when you believed something foolish, felt some strong, destructive emotion. Perhaps your enemy is the same, believing a foolish thing as we all have. Try to see the world through the eyes of your enemy. How did he become the enemy? What twisted him from the love and joy he experienced as a baby, as a toddler? Why did he go so wrong? Imagine you can understand that terrible path. Use your imagination and try to understand what might have twisted and corrupted your enemy, your persecutor. Try to explain to yourself how that might have happened. Write it down.

A: Altruistic Gift. The altruistic gift of forgiveness means that you forgive not because the person deserves it but rather because you have made some mistakes in your own life and would hope others would forgive you. Worthington says, "Have you ever harmed or offended a friend, a parent, or a partner who later forgave you? Think about your guilt. Then consider the way you felt when you were forgiven. Most people say, 'I felt free. The chains were broken.' Forgiveness can unshackle people from their interpersonal guilt. By recalling your own guilt and the gratitude over being forgiven, you can develop the desire to give that gift of freedom to the person who hurt you." *Write a letter* to the person who hurt you about how you want forgiveness yourself, and how you give because you wish to have that given to you.

This is the step from empathy (what made the perpetrator do it) to compassion (how I would want to be treated if I were the perpetrator). You build on compassion to forgive; you develop your compassion by forgiveness.

C: Commit to yourself that you will forgive. Promise yourself that you will. **Certify** that you have forgiven. *Make an actual **certificate** or letter attesting to your forgiveness of the other person. Tell others that you have forgiven the person you were angry with, and show them the certificate. *You do not* show the perpetrator the certificate.

I find that nearly always it is much safer to *not* tell the person you are forgiving of what you have achieved. Sometimes it is safe, but very rarely. If a hurtful person still has some ability to reach into your life and cause more harm, you should not tell them. It may tempt them to do you more damage.

If you have successfully developed the skill of compassion, you can see how you would not want a person to do further evil, since it will inevitably result in more suffering for that misguided soul. It is true compassion to try to prevent more evil in that person, since you reduce the burden of guilt they will have to eventually face.

H: Hold on to the forgiveness. When the memories come back – and naturally enough, they will come back – just recall the Certificate of Forgiveness, and remind yourself that you have already forgiven that. **Help** yourself by *writing* about how you have remembered that you have already forgiven. Keep remembering and reminding. "I let go of that, this is just an echo of something that I finished long ago."

Worthington suggests that some hurts will take several trips up the pyramid. Perhaps that will be true for you too. I have come to think that forgiveness is more a way of life than an single event. Like eating healthy food or exercise, it takes persistence and perseverance. The result is relief and joy.

Let me repeat a key point. Sometimes people fear forgiving an evil person because they very well might harm them again. This is a sensible position to take. Being forgiving doesn't mean you have to be foolish. If the angry or harmful person hasn't changed his ways, you would be silly to let your forgiveness make you do something risky, like trust an untrustworthy person. Forgiveness is a spiritual approach to life, but not a silly one. Do it because it makes the whole world a better place, and makes your own heart a better place for you to live. But always, be wise and cautious.

So you might forgive someone and never tell that person because your own deep wisdom, your best judgement, tells you that would be unwise. You forgive for the benefit and blessing it will be for you, as Tyler Perry says, and not necessarily to benefit that other person.

By the same token, suppose a vicious criminal damages you in some way, and you forgive that person. Still it would be important for the individual to go to prison, since that keeps him from hurting other people. Compassion for all people would demand that he be in prison as long as possible, reducing the damage he might do. You have forgiven him, but he is still accountable before the law.

Just as we all need to forgive, we all need forgiveness. St. Paul says in the Bible that we all are sinners and come short of the glory of God. To me, that is a comforting thought. It means I can look at every person in the world with compassion and understanding. From the greatest to the least, we are all human and we all make mistakes. Let us embrace the life of forgiveness.

What have we covered?

● Compassion are forgiveness are crucial happiness and healing skills.

● Resentment is clearly a hard-wired part of us.

● Skills of compassion help us rise above our hard-wired nature.

- *Recall* the pain.

- *Empathize* with the perpetrator.

- Activate the *Altruistic* gift of forgiveness.

- *Commit* to forgiving and *certify* you forgive.

- *Hold* onto forgiveness when resentment return.

● Be *very* cautious about telling perpetrators you have forgiven them. The perpetrator is still legally and ethically accountable, and it is to their benefit to be held accountable.

Try this: Keep a scrapbook of newspaper clipping about forgiveness. Over a year, you will be able to collect many stories of people who have forgiven great wrongs. These stories inspire us and elevate our feelings towards all people.

Relationships and
Contributing to the World

Chapter 9
Talents: Varieties of Happiness

In a report card note to the parents of Roberta Joan Anderson a few decades back, the sixth grade teacher at Queen Elizabeth School offered this starchy recommendation: "Joan should pay attention to other subjects than art."
– James Brooke, New York Times, Aug. 22, 2000
(Joni Mitchell, one of the greatest singer-songwriters of the twentieth century, never stopped paying attention to her art. Thank you, Joni.)

Rottweilers are great dogs. I once owned a Rottweiler. She was a gift from a young man who had discovered that his apartment contract didn't allow him to own a dog. (Long term planning for the young: twenty minutes from now.)

Rather than see her go to a pound, we adopted her. I was a jogger and took her running. We went by a field with some cattle, and that dog kept staring at the cows. It seemed to me that she was trying to recall something. After the run I got a book on Rottweilers and learned that it is a breed of dog developed by the Romans to herd cattle. The cattle spoke to this dog of who she truly was.

I was watching a TV special on Labrador retrievers, God's finest dog. A woman raises trout in a series of ponds. When she gets an order from a restaurant for fresh trout, her Labs jump into the ponds. They swim under water and "herd" the fish toward her net. She dips up the trout until she has filled the order. Labs were developed to swim underwater and free fishermen's nets that were stuck on the bottom of the ocean. This explains their hardy nature and willingness to jump into very cold water. Nowadays they serve in new ways. They retrieve ducks, as well as guide the blind and sniff out marijuana and bombs. They love to be of service, and are happiest when working, but water service is the best.

If you aren't sick of dog metaphors and are still with me, let's talk about who you are and what you are meant to be about. (Some people think a preposition isn't something you should end a sentence with. I am not of that school, obviously.)

Professor Chris Peterson (University of Michigan) and Professor Martin Seligman (U Penn; we've met him before) noticed a definite lack of diagnostic categories in the area of strengths. We have some pretty good diagnoses for weaknesses, including many flavors of depression, anxiety, drug and alcohol problems, psychosis . . . but few for strengths.

They undertook a huge project, to determine what kinds of strengths all societies and cultures value. They studied literature from all around the globe, and distilled the virtues that all cultures value. They identified twenty-four universal virtues. They then grouped those virtues into six general categories.

Why does this matter to you? Because this matter of virtues, of innate talents, turns out to be a key to happiness and high performance. You see, each person has a unique set of strengths. Mother Nature dislikes uniformity. Like the Labrador Retriever, when you are engaged in exercising your own virtues, you are happiest. A Greyhound has a different "calling" in life than the Lab. You have a different calling than your neighbor, and if your neighbor is true to his calling, and you are true to yours, you will both live happier lives.

The Six Virtue Categories

These six categories may or may not cover all the virtues you can think of. Recall that these are *universal* virtues, occurring in all cultures. I have taken these from Chris Peterson and Marty Seligman's 2003 book on virtues.

- Wisdom and Knowledge: the virtues of learning and applying information, insight, and good judgment.

- Courage: virtues of accomplishing goals when faced with serious obstacles, especially threatening obstacles. These may be *outer* or external, or *inner* or personal fears, insecurities, and mixed feelings.

- Love: reaching out to and befriending others, taking care of others.

- Justice: civic or community strengths that create a healthy group.

- Temperance: virtues that protect against unwise excess.

- Transcendence: strengths that connect to the larger universe, strengths that make life meaningful.

Take a minute and select the area that you think might be your personal focus. Which would be most like you? Maybe you can pick two areas, but I suggest you focus only on the strongest area for you. We can't be good at everything. Have you selected one or two that fit you? Good.

Now look at the individual strengths within each area, as Peterson and Seligman have defined them. You selected one or two categories. Now look at the specific virtues in each category that you selected. Pick one or two that you feel most connected with.

Rate each specific virtue on a 1-5 scale, with 1 = *not like me at all* and 5 = *most like me*. Those you rate at 5 are your unique combination of virtues.

WISDOM AND KNOWLEDGE:

Creativity/originality/ingenuity: Thinking of novel and productive ways to do things; Includes artistic achievement but is not limited to it.

Curiosity/interest/novelty-seeking/openness to experience: Taking an interest in all of ongoing experience; finding all subjects and topics fascinating; exploring and discovering.

Judgment/critical thinking/open-mindedness: Thinking things through and examining them from all sides; *not* jumping to conclusions; being able to change one's mind in light of evidence; weighing all evidence fairly.

Love of learning: Mastering new skills, topics, and bodies of knowledge, whether on one's own or formally. Obviously related to the strength of curiosity but goes beyond it to describe the tendency to add *systematically* to what one knows.

Perspective: Being able to provide wise counsel to others; having ways of looking at the world that make sense to the self and to other people.

COURAGE:

Bravery/valor: *Not* shrinking from threat, challenge, difficulty, or pain; speaking up for what is right even if there is opposition; acting on convictions even if unpopular; Includes physical bravery but is not limited to it.

Industry/perseverance/diligence: Finishing what one starts; persisting in a course of action in spite of obstacles; "getting it out the door"; taking pleasure in completing tasks.

Integrity/honesty/authenticity: Speaking the truth but more broadly presenting oneself in a genuine way; being without pretense; taking responsibility for one's feelings and actions.

Vitality/zest/enthusiasm: Approaching life with excitement and energy; *not* doing things halfway or halfheartedly; living life as an adventure; feeling alive and activated.

LOVE:

Intimacy/reciprocal attachment: Valuing close relations with others, in particular those in which sharing and caring are reciprocated; being close to people.

Kindness/generosity/nurturance: Doing favors and good deeds for others; helping them; taking care of them.

Social intelligence/personal intelligence/emotional intelligence: Being aware of the motives and feelings of other people and the self; knowing what to do to fit in to different social situations; knowing what makes other people tick.

JUSTICE:

Citizenship/duty/loyalty/teamwork: Working well as member of a group or team; being loyal to the group; doing one's share.

Equity/fairness: Treating all people the same according to notions of fairness and justice; *not* letting personal feelings bias decisions about others; giving everyone a fair chance .

Leadership: Encouraging a group of which one is a member to get things done and at the same time good relations within the group; organizing group activities and seeing that they happen.

TEMPERANCE:

Forgiveness/mercy: Forgiving those who have done wrong; giving people a second chance; *not* being vengeful

Modesty/humility: Letting one's accomplishments speak for themselves; *not* seeking the spotlight; *not* regarding one's self as more special than one is

Prudence/caution: Being careful about one's choices; *not* taking undue risks; *not* saying or doing things that might later be regretted

Self-control/self-regulation: Regulating what one feels and does; being disciplined; controlling one's appetites and emotions

TRANSCENDENCE:

Awe/wonder/appreciation of beauty and excellence: Noticing and appreciating beauty, excellence, and/or skilled performance in all domains of life, from nature to art to mathematics to science to everyday experience

Gratitude: Being aware of and thankful for the good things that happen; taking time to express thanks

Hope/optimism/future-mindedness: Expecting the best in the future and working to achieve it; believing that a good future is something that can be brought about

Playfulness/humor: Liking to laugh and tease; bringing smiles to other people; seeing the light side; making (not necessarily telling) jokes

Spirituality/sense of purpose/faith/religiousness: Having coherent beliefs about the higher purpose and meaning of the universe; knowing where one fits within the larger scheme; having beliefs about the meaning of life that shape conduct and provide comfort

Get a Second Opinion

Sometimes our own estimates are quite accurate, and sometimes they contain a certain amount of blindness. You could also ask someone who knows you well and loves or respects you to rate you on these twenty-four virtues and the six categories. Compare them.

Another option is to go to Seligman's amazing web site: http://www.authentichappiness.sas.upenn.edu/, and take a rather extensive test on these, the VIA (Values in Action) survey.

You may have already visited this site if you took his Optimism test. If not, Seligman has created a wonderful site focused on his research on happiness. You must register, but the test if free and you will get valuable feedback about your strengths and weak areas. It also offers a child version of the same test, which should be interesting to help children grow and develop.

Your Happiness Plan

There are two things you can do with this. Either will increase your personal happiness.

First, build on your areas of strength. Seligman and his associates have some very good evidence that when we make a conscious effort to put more energy into our strongest areas, we are happier. Like the Rottweiler who feels most at home around cattle or the Labrador finding joy in chasing fish, we feel we are truly who we are when we are playing to our strengths.

Second, University of Virginia psychologist Jon Haidt has found that people increase their happiness when they strive to improve an area of weakness. So both approaches work. Let's look at improving areas of weakness.

Psychologist Ben Dean shares an example of that. He tells of how he scored very low on the Transcendence category of Gratitude. But he knew that this virtue is a major contributor to happiness. So he made a plan to write down five things each day that he was grateful for, the Gratitude Diary we have talked about. He did that for a year and then re-took the VIA. He felt much more happy, and his score was now very high on Gratitude.

There is a third possible option, the Ben Franklin plan. Franklin listed certain virtues he wanted to cultivate. He listed thirteen of them, and then cultivated one each week for thirteen weeks, then rotated through them again after he came to the end. In this way, he thought that he could continually improve himself. Franklin was clearly the smartest man of his generation, and perhaps one of the smartest men of all time, and we should consider his approach.

So whether you work on a strength, a weakness, or follow the Franklin plan, let's talk about some ways to actually do that.

Expanding your talents and virtues will work best if you keep a journal. Write each night about what you did to work on your strengths. Pick the top two or three strengths in yourself and do something each day that "plays to" that strength.

Some virtues do produce more happiness than others. Zest, Hope, Curiosity, Forgiveness, and Love all raise happiness and resiliency nicely. If you see yourself as low in those, I suggest they be your focus.

Thanks to Jon Haidt, Ph.D. of the University of Virginia for an earlier version of this list.

WISDOM AND KNOWLEDGE

Creativity, ingenuity and originality

- Create a picture, a poem, or a musical composition.
- Submit a piece to a literary magazine or newspaper.
- Brainstorm ways to do your daily work in new ways.
- Pick one common object and devise a new use for it.

Curiosity and Interest in the World

- Ask questions of people you meet about their lives, their interests, their insights.
- Discover new places, explore in your town region, or state.
- Explore the stacks in a library; browse widely, or skim an interesting looking book each day.
- Go to a meeting or hear a speaker.

Love of Learning

- Discover one new place in town and spend time exploring it.
- Read a newspaper or magazine you have never picked up before.
- Ask a question of someone you admire.
- Research a topic you've always found intriguing but never found the time to learn more about.

Judgment, Critical Thinking and Open-Mindedness

- Go to a multi-cultural group or event.
- Play devil's advocate and discuss an issue from the side opposite

to your personal views.

- Take a colleague out to lunch who is different from you in some way and learn about his / her point of view.
- Go to a different church or religious event or political gathering.
- Pick something you believe strongly, and think about how you might be wrong. Ask yourself how you would know if you *were* wrong.

Perspective (Wisdom)

- Get a quote a day online. Collect and review these points of wisdom.
- Think of the wisest person you know. Interview them about how they became wise. Try to live each day as that person would live.
- Read historical biographies and see where famous people were both wise and foolish.

COURAGE

Bravery or valor

- Do something physically safe but frightening or challenging.
- Speak up in groups or volunteer to speak publically, if you don't normally.
- Stand up for someone even if you disagree with him/her.
- Introduce yourself to a stranger, if you tend to shyness.
- Speak up for an unpopular idea you believe in.

Industry, diligence and perseverance

- Finish work ahead of time.
- Recognize your thoughts about stopping a task, and choose to ignore them. Focus on the task at hand.
- Plan ahead – use a calendar for assignments and meetings.
- In the morning, make a list of things that you want to get done that day that could be put off. Finish them that day.

Integrity, honesty, genuineness

- Refrain from telling small white lies to friends (including insincere compliments). Try to be brutally frank about yourself. If you do tell a lie or misrepresent yourself, admit it and apologize right away.
- Look for times you have been wrong. Publically admit it.
- Speak truthfully to others about the things you admire or value in them.
- Notice times when you inhibit yourself because you are afraid of what others will think. Resolve to speak frankly in the future.
- At the end of each day, identify something you did that showed honesty or genuineness and appreciate yourself for that.

Zest, Enthusiasm, and Energy

- Go out of your way to become more involved in an organization.
- Smile much more than you are used to, especially if it feels uncomfortable or phony.

- Take up a greater interest in others' work, i.e., volunteer to help them in a project.
- Savor. While eating or drinking something, concentrate on the taste and sensations. Try to appreciate every aspect of that food or drink.
- Do something physically vigorous in the morning (e.g., jog, push-ups).
- Speak and move more quickly than you are used to.

LOVE

Capacity to Love and be Loved
- Tell a special person that you love them.
- Show love to family members (card, note, flowers . . .).
- Send a friend a card or e-card to say that you were thinking about him/her.
- Give loved ones a big hug and a kiss
- When someone shows love for you, savor the moment. Focus on the pleasure of being cared about. Drink it up.

Kindness and generosity
- Leave a large tip for a small check.
- Do a random act of kindness every day (a simple, small favor). Make it anonymous if possible.
- Be a listening ear to a friend. Ask them how their day was and

actually listen to the answer before telling them about your own day.

- Send an e-card or a kind note to a different friend each day.

Social Intelligence

- Introduce yourself to people.
- Go into a party with people you don't know and try to make some friends.
- Whenever you talk with someone, try to figure out what his or her motives and concerns are, what virtues he / she has.
- Look for someone who is alone and make an effort to speak with them.

JUSTICE

Citizenship and Teamwork

- Volunteer at a school.
- Take on added responsibility within an organization you are already a part of (also increases Zest).
- Pick up litter that you see on the ground.
- Organize a neighborhood dinner.
- Organize a volunteer group in your neighborhood.

Fairness Equity and Justice

- Allow someone to speak their piece while keeping an open mind by not passing judgment.

- Stay impartial in an argument between friends despite your beliefs (be the impartial mediator).
- Notice when you treat someone based on a stereotype or pre-conception; deliberately practice the opposite.

Leadership

- Organize some special activity for your friends.
- Plan an outing or trip for a group of friends. Make assignments. Follow up. Make it happen.
- Organize a study group, book club, or a volunteer group in your neighborhood.
- Volunteer to be a Boy Scout or Girl Scout leader.

TEMPERANCE

Forgiveness and Mercy

- Think of someone who has offended you. Try to see the situation from their perspective. Follow the Forgiveness model in this book.
- Make contact with someone who has made you mad in the past. Let them know that you forgive them, or just be kind to them in your conversation.
- When someone does something that you do not understand, try to fathom his or her intentions in the actions.

Modesty

- Don't talk about yourself at all for a full day. If people ask about you, answer briefly and then focus your interest onto them.
- Dress and act modestly, so as not to attract attention to yourself. Reduce jewelry as much as you can. Imagine you are trying to simply blend in, and dress accordingly.
- Notice someone doing something well, better than you could do it. Give that person a sincere compliment.

Self-Control and Self-Regulation
- Set aside an hour (or other designated amount of time) and work on a project in a quiet, private place.
- Work out four days a week or more. Keep up a routine.
- Clean or organize your home. Every day, make sure that you pick up whatever mess you made during the day.
- Make a resolution to not gossip. When you feel the urge to talk about someone behind his or her back, remember your resolution and stop yourself before you talk.
- When you get overly emotional about something, calm down and consider the issues again.

Caution, Prudence and Discretion
- Notice when you are tempted to do something that makes you a bit uneasy. Ask yourself how you will feel an hour later? A week later? A month later?
- Review your insurance, will, and financial plan.

- Keep secrets, especially juicy ones.
- Check your car tires, oil, radiator and so on before going for a drive.
- Prepare and maintain an emergency kit with basic supplies to help you survive for three days without outside help. Put it in a duffle bag where you can grab it in a moment.
- Set aside in your home or apartment, basic food for three months, water for two weeks (around fourteen gallons per person) and clothing for harsh conditions.
- Have an emergency supply of cash that you never touch for ordinary expenses.
- Cut down or cut out credit cards. Pay off debts early.

TRANSCENDENCE

Appreciation of Beauty and Excellence
- Go to a museum and pick out a piece of artwork or a display that has aesthetic value and touches you because of its beauty.
- Take a walk with a friend and comment appreciatively on what you see.
- Pick out the most moving music you know of, and listen to it appreciatively on headphones every night. Or ask a friend to recommend the most beautiful music he or she knows.
- Keep a journal, and every night, record something you saw during the day that struck you as extremely beautiful, or skillful.
- Find something that makes you happy, in aesthetics or value, a

physical activity or an object, and let it inspire you throughout the day.

Gratitude

- Keep a journal, and each night, make a list of three to five things that you are thankful for that day.
- Every day, thank someone for something that you might otherwise take for granted (e.g., thanking the janitor who cleans your office).
- Say "thank you" more often, to more people.
- Call a parent/sibling/friend each day and thank him/her (e.g., for helping you to become who you are, or for always being there for you). Write a "thank you letter" and deliver it.
- Send someone a "thank you" note.

Hope, Optimism, and Future-Mindedness

- When you are in a bad situation, turn it around to see the optimistic side of it. You can almost always find some good in a situation, regardless of how awful it seems at the time.
- Reflect on bad decisions you have made. What did you learn? Forgive yourself and move on in life realizing that you cannot go backwards, only focus on the present and future.
- Notice your negative thoughts. Counter them with at least three to four positive thoughts.
- Reaffirm yourself that you can and will succeed at whatever you

put your mind to. Imagine yourself accomplishing your goals.

Spirituality and Sense of Purpose, and Faith
- Daily, think about the purpose of life, and where you fit in.
- Pray morning and night.
- Read a religious or spiritual book.
- Attend religious services often.
- Spend a few minutes a day in meditation or contemplating a virtue you would like to develop.

Humor and Playfulness
- Every day, make someone smile or laugh.
- Learn a joke a day and tell it to your friends.
- Watch a funny movie or TV show.
- Write a silly letter to the editor.
- Learn a magic trick and perform it for your friends.

Using a similar list of suggestions, Haidt asked students to work on one area of weakness. He learned that their level of satisfaction rose when they improved. Seligman has found that when you work on increasing an area of strength, your happiness level also improves. As I mentioned earlier, either approach works. You may take your pick.

What have we covered?
● We identified six general areas of virtue, truly valued by all cultures.
● We defined twenty-four specific virtues.
● You are unique in your combination of innate virtues, your areas of strength. If you increase the energy you put into your talents, you will be happier.
● Some virtues contribute more to happiness. If you are low in those virtues and work to increase them, you will be happier.

Try this: Figure out the virtues in people around you, friends, co-workers, your children, or your spouse. Compliment them on those talents, and notice what effect your appreciation makes for them.

Chapter 10
Social Connections

We cannot live for ourselves alone. Our lives are connected by a thousand invisible threads, and along these sympathetic fibers, our actions run as causes and return to us as results.
– Herman Melville

Happiness researchers assume there are no happy hermits. That is based on the realization that without significant exception, truly happy people are well connected people. They like others and others like them. They reach out to others and like to form friendships.

Whether you are an introvert who cherishes a few good friends, or an extravert who is able to nurture and maintain many friends, connection counts. Let's talk about improving those connections.

Subversive Secret

What if there were a secret that could devastate the marriage counseling industry? What if it could vastly improve your marriage, your family life? What if it could virtually insure that you'd never have to go through the pain of a divorce?

Well, I am not sure I should go that far. But I will tell you the secret. It has to do with your purpose in relationships. If you are (or ever have been) married, you probably can recall the reason you got married. The person you were about to marry seemed like the ideal person for you, someone who would complete you, would meet your needs, someone who would bring out the best in you. Your purpose was to be loved and return that love to a perfect being, your soul mate.

But it didn't quite last, did it? There is a Chinese saying: "If you want to be happy for three months, get married." That seems to bear out pretty well. The happiness doesn't last, and reality sets in. Biologists tell us that the oxytocin hormone

> *When studying very happy people, there is not one who is not highly connected with other people. Happy people are social.*
> – Dr. Ed Diener, happiness researcher

that causes us to bond to each other only lasts for about a year at the most, so if you were engaged for a year, that intense bonding of oxytocin is pretty much finished. So now that same person, the person who seemed to complete you, now annoys and irritates you. Their idiosyncracies that were so heart-warming are now horrible character flaws that should be eliminated. Beauty fades and the richness of the love you had flees.

Nothing is as it should be.

Welcome to the world of the adult relationship. Things never are quite as they should be. So what is to be done? One solution, one that half of our population adopts, is to divorce the evil villain that you were foolish enough to marry, and start to seek out your Soul Mate. Of course, it doesn't occur to you that your soul mate might find you as flawed and annoying as you find your current spouse. The poet e.e. cummings once said, "unbeing returns upon one's unself, space being curved," and so it is that we tend to repeat variations on our relationship mistakes.

How can this be changed? How can we keep this bad karma from our previous mistakes from returning to haunt us like a hungry ghost wanting to dine upon our souls?

The subversive secret is in our purpose. Your job in a relationship is not to be pleased and have your needs met. Your job is not to meet the other person's needs. Your job is simply to enjoy the person you are with.

You may ask, is that it? Yes, that is all there is to it. If you refocus your intentions, you change the whole world. If your intentions are that the other person should be meeting your needs, you are trying to control the other

Your job in a relationship is not to have your needs met. Your job is not to meet the other person's needs. Your job is simply to enjoy the person you are with. All flows from that.

person. That cannot be done. When you try, the other person pushes back, creating a negative downward spiral. You try to manipulate or direct your partner, and the partner resists that direction, becoming rigid and less responsive. You criticize your partner, and the partner pushes back, denying, resisting, or criticizing you in turn. Escalation. One pushing, the other pushing back. It becomes impossible to decide who pushed first. All we can see is the emotional death spiral.

You're on the wrong train of thought, imagining that your partner is supposed to meet your needs. Transform your intention. Change trains. "My job is to enjoy the person I am with," you affirm. Like learning to play a musical instrument, it takes will and practice. You have to become aware of when you are not achieving your goal. If you listen to yourself, you hear when you are off key, when your meter is off, and you practice and practice until you can do it right. Remember K. Anders Ericcson's studies of experts. The only difference was *deliberate practice*. That means the expert analyzes where she is not up to her own standard, and engages in conscious, mindful practice until she is very skilled.

"My job," you repeat to yourself, "is to enjoy the person I am with right now." Your skillful practice of that attitude will yield rich returns.

The Appreciation Key

Now lift your eyes beyond this narrow matter of marriage. When we broaden our vision, we see this principle is generally true. All relationships benefit from your skill at appreciating other people. Surveys by the Gallup organization showed clearly that the supervisor is key to high performance in workgroups. When that supervisor is a positive person who sees the good in others, the workgroup is stable and productive. When the supervisor believes his job is to criticize his workers, the group is unstable. People don't work as hard. They are all trying to figure out how to get a different job!

Leadership means influencing people, but how much better is the leader who influences through inspiration, through bringing out the best in us! When you practice this key, the skill of appreciating others, you are able to lift and inspire.

If you are not a formal, designated leader, you still influence. We all have impact on each other. When you sense that people enjoy being around you, that you energize others because your eye is full of valuing and appreciation, you will feel profoundly positive.

Skillful Practice: Reframing

You might try our useful tool of reframing as a skill to help yourself with that. We spoke of this when we discussed the gratitude diary. Again, our focus here shifts from helping our inner state to helping our relationships. When we appreciate even the "bad" behavior of those around us, that will energize our compassion and inspire them.

• Think of a *circumstance* in which the behavior is appropriate, e.g., "While I can understand how your daughter's stubbornness is extremely irritating, have you considered how comforted you can feel from that when you realize how she can use that stubbornness when she is with a person trying to talk her into doing something harmful to herself?"

• Discover a *positive intention* underlying the "bad" behavior. For example, smoking cigarettes is a bad habit, we all agree. But behind that bad habit is a positive hope of feeling more relaxed or fitting in with one's friends. Ironically, I found that clients are more able to stop the smoking habit when they actually appreciate the good intent behind it.

• Reframe the sequences of behavior. For example: While you can understandably feel that your wife's (or husband's) criticism makes you defensive, we really cannot be sure whether that it true, or whether in fact your defensiveness makes your wife (husband) criticize you. It is quite possible that when you defend yourself, you are criticized.

• Look for a hidden benefit, "Of course your husband's snoring bothers you; but at least you are sure he is alive!"

As If Experiments

Another skillful practice is to act *as if* you were pleased and thrilled with others. While this raises the danger of acting in a phony or insincere way, we could also see it as skill practice. The anthropologist Gregory Bateson told about a colleague who studied the Japanese culture after World War II. This man particularly studied Japanese families. After studying one family in which the father seemed to be an immature and impulsive man, he was conducting exit interviews. He met with the two daughters and observed to them, "You both seem to greatly respect your father." The girls looked at each other in surprise. "Oh no," they replied, "we don't respect him at all."

"Then why," asked the anthropologist, "do you both do such

respectful bows and use the respectful terms of address to him?"

"We are practicing respect," they explained, "so that when we meet people we do respect, we are skillful at showing it."

If you practice respect, compassion, and warmth when people don't deserve it, you will be a tremendous success at showing appreciation to those who do.

Imagine yourself unhappy over another person. The individual is acting in some way that you object to. Maybe he ends sentences with the preposition "to." No class whatsoever.

In any case, now imagine the problem is totally corrected. That same person has completely changed his behavior. You see that change. How does it help? Rise above the situation and see how you would change your behavior. What do you now do that you didn't do before? Imagine as if you were watching a video, kind of like a reality show on T.V.

Suppose the video didn't even show his behavior, only your own? How would you be able to tell, just by watching yourself, that the change had already happened?

Now you simply make an inner resolve, a commitment to act as if the change had already happened. Rather than waiting for your friend to change, take charge. Change your own behavior. Notice how your feelings change. Notice whether the other person also changes.

Write in your journal about the results.

Assertive and Constructive

Studies on happy marriages found an interesting and important pattern. People in families can respond either *assertively* or *passively*. They can respond *constructively* or *critically*.

Let's say a husband comes home from work and announces he has been laid off.

An assertive and constructive response would be something with both empathy and encouragement. "What a shock! That must have hit you hard. I want you to know I am confident that you will bounce back quickly."

Assertive and critical? There would be both no empathy and a negative expectation about the future. "Well, what did you do wrong? They didn't close the whole plant, it must be that you let them down. You will probably take forever to get another job."

Passive and constructive? Well, imagine little empathy and a slightly positive response. "Well, I guess I can try to get extra work myself to help us through."

Passive and critical? Perhaps changing the topic, such as "Yeah, I guess you had a bad day, but mine was worse."

The only pattern associated with very happy marriages was the assertive and constructive pattern. Obviously, the critical or negative responses are always bad, and passive is always bad. If you notice yourself responding this way, you may want to rethink your habit.

Symmetrical and Complimentary

Equals don't give each other orders. A symmetrical relationship is one in which we treat each other with respect. We do not have the authority to say, "You should, you ought to, you have to . . ." Instead we have to say, "Would you consider, could you do me the favor, are you able to help me with this?"

A complimentary relationship is one in which one person has accountability for the actions of the other. A sergeant commands a private to do an act. If the private doesn't do that act, the sergeant is accountable to the company commander.

Our children are (or at least, they should be) in a complimentary relationship to us. They want to be symmetrical even when it is not reasonable, and we frequently have a real struggle keeping that from happening. It is reasonable to say, "You must, you have to" to children. As they get older, we naturally move away from complimentary relationships to symmetrical. My mother told me what to do when I was a child. Now she asks me for help but doesn't command. She intuitively understands this principle.

Now what kind of relationship should a husband and wife have? I believe it should be symmetrical. It is inappropriate for you to give your spouse orders; you are the equal, not the boss. A lasting relationship in marriage is based on respect, a symmetrical relationship in which each offers to the other, but the other may refuse the offer.

"But how will decisions get made?" bleat those who don't understand this rule. "Somebody has to be in charge!" The poet Robert Frost said "Something there is that doesn't like a wall," and built into us at a very deep level is a kind of resistance to being ordered around. As humans we are tuned into who is our superior and who is our equal, and to as great an extent as possible, we want equality and not superior-inferior relationships.

If you want a happy marriage, you simply must understand that you and your spouse are equals. If you can achieve this understanding, you will be happier.

Your Gratitude Diary

We have covered this before. This exercise helps people become more optimistic, as we said. But it also helps you become better connected. Write in your journal or diary each gratitude toward friends and neighbors, people at work, people you meet at the club or at your church. Try to expand your circle of gratitude until it encompasses more and more people.

When you do that, your appreciative feelings leak out. Others become aware of them, and they are pleased with your appreciation of them. This brings out the best in them. Sometimes the very problem we cannot tolerate is a reaction to our own behavior. We are criticizing and judging the other person and not bringing out the best in them.

Think of a cold-warm continuum. When we are critical and judging, we are *cold*. The human body is 60% water. If that water gets cold, people get rigid. They turn to ice. Not good for relationships.

When you warm up the

> *"Gratitude is a fruit of great cultivation; you do not find it among gross people"*
> – Samuel Johnson

relationship, the water turns fluid again. Liquid is flexible, and can change in a moment. It can flow around obstacles and smooth them. Water is better off fluid. So are relationships.

Gratitude Visit

Another antidote for depression, the gratitude visit, also connects you with others. Write a letter of thanks to someone you feel grateful towards. Now laminate that letter, visit the person, and read it to them. Leave your laminated gratitude letter behind. Studies found that such a visit raised the happiness level of the writer for several weeks after that. If you would improve your social connections, try this simple experiment.

Service Diary

A study of raising happiness in college students found that those who performed service, acts of charity and generosity, became much happier. In this experiment, students would emphasize hedonism, enjoyment of life through pleasure, excitement, and entertainment for one week, and service for the next week. The service week resulted in much higher levels of happiness.

One student was with her group who had just finished helping a widow paint and fix up her house. They were all feeling good, riding home together in a car, and suddenly one of the students called for the car to stop. She assumed he was near his home, but instead he jumped out and ran to a parked car. A woman was trying to change a flat tire and he began helping her. Seeing him do that, she reported, filled her with a kind of joy and excitement. She felt inspired, lifted up by seeing this spontaneous act. She felt almost giddy.

Sonja Lyubomirsky's studies on service support this. People who tried to take one day a week for performing acts of kindness were likely to raise their happiness level significantly. On a weekend, set aside a day for service to others.

As you write down acts of kindness, you are reliving them and making such acts more likely in your own future. Once a week or so, jot down all the things you have done that were helpful to other people. Especially try to perform anonymous acts, where there is no way that you can be paid back for your charity.

The key here seems to be in service that cannot be repaid. If you give service and keep a mental account, you are likely to be disappointed. So try to serve anonymously, or at least in ways where you cannot expect any repayment.

What have we covered?

● Increasing social connection will raise happiness.

● Reframing your attitude about people, from expecting others to please you to thinking of being pleased as a skill you exercise is key.

● When others give you good news, response *assertively and constructively.*

● Emphasize symmetrical relationships; treat others as equals, not as servants.

● Gratitude diaries and gratitude letters increase connection.

● Serving others raises happiness, especially when it is done anonymously or in a situation where no pay-back is expected or even possible.

Try this: Smile at other people. Set as your personal goal to get a smile from others you associate with. See if showing that appreciation for them makes them connect with you much more.

Chapter 11
Happiness at Work

I know the price of success: dedication, hard work, and an unremitting devotion to the things you want to see happen.
– Frank Lloyd Wright

D o what you enjoy, and if you can't do that, then enjoy what you do. We spend so much of our day at work, and often we get so much satisfaction from work that it would be foolish not to think about skills of enjoying work. Crosby, Stills, Nash and Young (a folk-rock band of the 1960s) sang, "If you can't be with the one you love, then love the one you're with."

I am going to let you in on a secret. Enjoying work is a skill, not something you are born with. Like any skill, the more you practice it the more you will like it. Too often people have the attitude that they should just naturally enjoy what they are doing, and then they would be happy. But all work can be tiresome or tedious or uncomfortable. There are few perfect jobs in this world. I recall an interview with a forest ranger, the director of Yellowstone National Park. The interviewer asked this forest ranger about his job satisfaction. He said it was low. The job was too stressful, what with all the paperwork and managing all the rangers in the park. You can see the role of habituation in this story. We save our money to go to Yellowstone, and are in awe of its majesty. He is around it every day and it is just another job. I suppose that for vacation he would go to a busy city to unwind.

On the other hand, yesterday I hired a man to come to our mountain cabin and pump out the outhouse. That wouldn't seem to be a very pleasant job, would it? But he seemed to enjoy his work, and remembered being at that cabin when another family owned it. He chatted very pleasantly about sports and politics and the coming winter season. He was an easy person to be with.

The Secret to Job Happiness

So why is the forest ranger unhappy and the sewer pumping service operator happy? What if the first man is simply unskilled at happiness at work and the second is skilled? Could there be a secret to being happy?

There could be. In fact, there is. It has to do entirely

Counter-factual thinking is wishing things were different, you were somewhere else, doing something else. You wish the past were different and you had made other choices. It is a sure pathway to misery.

128

with our habits of thinking. Certain trains of thought lead us to a station of personal work satisfaction, and others lead to a different station. As you step onto one train or another, you are accepting the destination to which that train takes you.

Suppose you think about how you would rather be doing something else. This is called *counter factual thinking*, the tendency to deny reality and wish it were something else. A train of thought comes through the station of your conscious mind. Its destination is distraction, counter factual thinking, and unhappiness. The train looks something like "I wish I could be doing . . ." or perhaps "I hate this job because . . ."

The great secret is that just because a thought comes through your awareness, you don't have to follow that thought. You can drop it. You can simply refuse to pursue it. You can comment to yourself, "Well, that thought doesn't go anywhere that I want to go." The train may seem important, but if you refuse to get on, that train will move on and out of your awareness. You simply drop the thought.

Then you can practice having a quiet mind. You can focus on your experience at the moment. Focusing on the present moment brings peace and pleasure.

What's Good about Your Work?

All productive work, all work that is in demand, involves helping other people. As I suggested in the last chapter, the need to be of service is built into you, in some very deep way. You connect to people through service. So focus on the service you perform. How does your work help?

My son had a job selling window shades. He had mixed feelings about that, thinking at times that it wasn't very dignified work. I argued the opposite. We bought some of his shades and they greatly enhanced the ambiance of our family room. I pointed out to him that he had made the home a more pleasant place. He contributed by improving people's living space.

If you focus your thinking on how your work serves and helps others, it will give you a clearer vision of your contribution.

Every legitimate job serves others. How does your job help? How do you bless the lives of others in what you do?

Customer Service

We all have stories of horrible customer service. It is all too easy. Just ask a group of friends about bad customer service and you'll get an earful. But what about great customer service? What themes do you hear in those stories? When you have received some unusually good customer service, doesn't it create a permanent sense of loyalty?

I was working for a Canadian client and meeting with employees in Calgary. I was staying at the Calgary Marriott. At lunch time, I broke the group and sent them out, and I wandered over to the hotel restaurant. A woman, the hostess for the restaurant, was trying to cope with a long line of large loud men. She asked me my name and how many in my party. "Johnson, one" I replied. After a few minutes she called me, "Mr.

Johnson, table for one."

The lunch was pretty good, so at the end of the day when I had dismissed the group I again strolled over to the restaurant. The same woman was there. As I walked in, she said, "Good evening, Mr. Johnson, table for one?" I was amazed that she recalled my name.

The next morning for breakfast the large loud men were back, and this time they had their wives. I learned from chatting with them that they were Shriners from Alabama, Georgia, and Mississippi, having a great time at a Calgary convention. The same hostess was there. Finally she got to me, and again to my surprise she recalled my name. I asked her, "How do you do that, recall my name?" She said that it was just a gift she seemed to have. I suspect that it was a gift she had rigorously practiced.

When you check out of a Marriott hotel, they give you a card and ask you to write any suggestions on it. I wrote, "Give Noelle in the restaurant a raise. Whatever you are paying her, it is not enough."

We now know that when you are in a good mood, you learn more and retain it better. At the time, it was Noelle's memory that impressed me. As I think about it now, it is more the underlying pleasant and cheerful demeanor that is key.

Customer service? Certainly it is a key to success in your career. If you are genuinely helpful to customers, whether inside the company or outside, you will be recognized as a person who should be given a raise, no matter what they are paying you. I think the key is not so much learning to do extra things, it is rather the core emotional state you create for yourself. Noelle may have practiced her memory feats, and they were impressive. But more important was a quiet positive emotional climate she created around her.

In your gratitude diary, be sure to write down times when you have given very good customer service to someone. Take some pride in what you have done.

Your own happiness is the master key to customer service. When you are happier, your customers sense it and are blessed.

Practice it so as to get consistently and consciously skilled. Cultivate real appreciation for the people around you, the customers, your co-workers, your subordinates. See if you can bring a smile to the faces of others, and then set that as a personal goal. Count the number of smiles you create in others.

Career Advancement

Dr. Mihaly Csikszentmihalyi (pronounced "Mike Chick-sent-me-high") investigated people who were unusually good at what they did. A number of them said when they were working at their best, they seemed to be carried along, as if by a current. He called this state "flow."

Csikszentmihalyi identifies the following as accompanying an experience of flow:

1. Clear goals (expectations and rules are discernible and goals are attainable and align appropriately with one's skill set and abilities).

2. Concentrating and focusing, a high degree of concentration on a limited field (a person engaged in the activity will have the opportunity to

focus and to delve deeply into it).

3. A loss of the feeling of self-consciousness, the merging of action and awareness.

4. Distorted sense of time, one's subjective experience of time is altered.

5. Direct and immediate feedback (successes and failures in the course of the activity are apparent, so that behavior can be adjusted as needed).

6. Balance between ability level and challenge (the activity is neither too easy nor too difficult).

7. A sense of personal control over the situation or activity.

8. The activity is intrinsically rewarding, so there is an effortlessness of action.

9. People become absorbed in their activity, and focus of awareness is narrowed down to the activity itself, action and awareness merging effortlessly.

You can see that many of these are under your own personal control. When you can achieve flow states, time passes unnoticed. Your productivity effortlessly improves. When I was young, I made a living as a carpenter, building houses. As I was learning my trade, I bent a lot of nails. (This was before the nail guns used today.) I discovered something. When I was hammering a nail, sometimes I was thinking about something else, like what else I could do for a living. But when I looked intently and steadily at the nail head, I was able to easily drive it home in two or three hits. Sometimes I could drive a 16d nail in a single blow! Focus, I discovered, is under my control, and I can focus on whatever I am doing. But if my attention wandered, my performance did too.

What will your boss or supervisor or customers think about you if you cultivate flow? It is clear that you can achieve flow in any job you want, by trying to raise your skills and increase at the same time the challenge of the job. Your boss notices, and before long, you are given more opportunities, greater responsibilities. If you view this new job as another opportunity to learn to experience flow, then again you move up in the organization. Forget yourself and you will find the rewards flow to you.

Your job is to enjoy the job you have right now. When you are quite good at that, a new job will open up. Now you don't know how to do that new job, do you? Great! You are being paid to learn!

Your job is to enjoy the job you have right now. When you are quite good at that, a new job or a new aspect of your job will open up. Now you don't know how to do that new job, do you? There are new things about it, and it may be somewhat a strain to achieve proficiency with the new job. Just look at it (reframe it) as a privilege. You are being paid to learn! Learn the new job and master it. Focus on the job today, what you are doing at this moment. Dismiss the irrelevant thoughts about what others are doing, or whether others are being paid more or better recognized. Just focus on your job today. Soon you will be in the flow experience we talked about earlier.

Soon another opportunity will come your way. Accept that with the understanding that you don't know how to do this new job either. You are being paid to learn. And once again, focus your attention totally on what you are doing, not on what you wish you were doing.

Pumping Outhouses

As our sewer truck driver was getting ready to leave, I asked him what he liked about his job. He spoke of the beautiful cabins in the mountains and how they would be impossible without him. He saw himself as making it possible for people to have cabins. He saw himself as providing a vital service, and he is right. We could not have the cabin unless we had a way to pump the outhouse. He is key to that.

"See you next year," he called to me as he drove away.

That man kept his focus. The temptation to lose our focus and wander off, thinking about yesterday or tomorrow, is always with us. Practice being present. Our brains are never fully developed. Even the Dalai Lama still meditates every day.

What have we covered?

● Enjoying your job is a skill.

● All legitimate jobs serve others. Focus on how your job helps people. Enjoy your customers.

● Flow comes when you raise your job skills and raise the challenge.

● When you practice focus and engagement in your job, new challenges will appear.

TRY THIS: Note in your diary people you meet that seems to deeply enjoy their job, such as my outhouse pumping friend. Ask them what they enjoy about their job and how they came to have it.

Chapter 12
Spirituality and Happiness

Nothing worth doing is completed in our lifetime,
  Therefore, we are saved by hope.
Nothing true or beautiful or good makes complete
sense in any immediate context of history;
  Therefore, we are saved by faith.
Nothing we do, however virtuous, can be accomplished
alone.
  Therefore, we are saved by love.
No virtuous act is quite as virtuous from the standpoint
of our friend or foe as from our own;
  Therefore, we are saved by the final form of love
which is forgiveness.
  – Reinhold Niebuhr

What role does spirituality play in happiness? In the United States, most people believe in a spiritual reality of some kind, such as belief in God, the reality of a spirit or soul within us, and the likelihood of life after death. However, in the past few years there have been several best-selling books attacking belief in God and the practice of religion. So what does the evidence say? What impact does belief have on happiness?

The easiest answer to this is that it all depends. It depends on how we see spirit, God, and ourselves.

Views of God

All polls agree that roughly 95% of Americans believe in God. Approximately 80% view themselves as Christian, of one flavor or another. But that really doesn't tell us what effect the belief in God has on one.

In 2005, Baylor University sponsored an extensive study of how we perceive God. If we exclude the 5.2% of Americans who don't believe in any God at all, we have four general views. Read each definition used in this study, and think about which one you agree with.

• The Authoritarian God: Individuals who believe in the Authoritarian God tend to think that God is highly involved in their daily lives and world affairs. They tend to believe that God helps them in their decision-making and is also responsible for global events such as economic upturns or tsunamis. They also tend to feel that God is quite angry and is capable of meting out punishment to those who are unfaithful or ungodly."

• Benevolent God: "Like believers in the Authoritarian God, believers in a Benevolent God tend to think that God is very active in our daily lives. But these individuals are less likely to believe that God is angry and acts in wrathful ways. Instead, the Benevolent God is mainly a force of positive influence in the world and is less willing to condemn or punish individuals."

• Critical God: "Believers in a Critical God feel that God really does not interact with the world. Nevertheless, God still observes the world and views the current state of the world unfavorably. These individuals feel that God's displeasure will be felt in another life and that divine justice may not be of this world."

• Distant God: "Believers in a Distant God think that God is not active in the world and not especially angry either. These individuals tend towards thinking about God as a cosmic force which set the laws of nature in motion. As such, God does not "do" things in the world and does not hold clear opinions about our activities or world events."

From those definitions, Baylor researchers created a set of questions to categorize people into these groups. The results were:
- Authoritarian God: 31.4%
- Benevolent God: 23%
- Critical God: 16%
- Distant God: 24.4%

We have to be careful with categories. After all, we know there are three kinds of people, those who know how to count, and those who don't. Suppose you think God is mostly benevolent and kind of authoritarian? Nevertheless, in terms of happiness, it would seem like a good bet to be a believer in the Benevolent version. But actually, either the authoritarian or benevolent image of God seems to make people much happier. People with the Critical and Distant view of God were not very happy. So it is the concept that there is a God involved with the world that creates a positive mood. Even if you think God is kind of strict, the involvement is what makes you happier. Thinking that God is distant from our present world is not much benefit.

Benefits of Church Attendance

In fact, religious people generally are much happier than those without any religion or spiritual practice. In 2006, Pew Research Center reported on a happiness survey which found that the more a person attends church, the happier she is.

Now I purposely said "she" in the paragraph above, because it turns out that women benefit more than men when it comes to enjoying religion. One study found that women who left church attendance were much more likely to become depressed, but men didn't seem affected in the same way. Men are also happier in religious practice, but women benefit more.

What's the Reason?

Several things play into religion and spirituality when it comes to happiness. Maybe happy people are more attracted to religion? This is possible but we cannot say for sure. More likely, there are some reason why people who are attending become happier. For example:

1. Religion and spirituality give one strong, stable views about the world, the future, and other people. Having clear and stable beliefs do seem to help one be happier.

2. Socializing helps. We do know that happy people like to socialize and that when we get depressed people out socializing, they do become happier. Church attendance is an ideal way to meet and socialize with people. Women benefit more from socializing than men do, and that may be why, when a woman loses her faith and doesn't replace it with another one, she does suffer more.

3. Service to others gives us a sense of joy and connection, and churches often promote various kinds of service. Raising money for disaster relief, volunteering for community service, even teaching a Sunday School class all speak to this need we have to be altruistic, to be interested in something besides ourselves.

4. Transcendental experiences are infrequent but do happen. People who attend church are likely to have moments of being at one with the universe. These moments of joy will keep one content for a long time.

So, for whatever reason, if you want more happiness, consider increasing your spirituality and religious practices.

Spirituality is . . .

A simple way to think about spirituality is (1) a sense of connection with the divine, along with (2) an awareness of your own triumph over your selfish side. One trusted teacher told me that since God owns everything in the universe, the only thing we can really give Him is our own hearts. When we rise above self-interest, we increase connection with the divine.

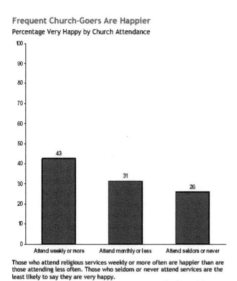

Frequent Church-Goers Are Happier
Percentage Very Happy by Church Attendance

Those who attend religious services weekly or more often are happier than are those attending less often. Those who seldom or never attend services are the least likely to say they are very happy.

PewResearchCenter

Prayer and meditation, reading spiritual sources, associating with spiritual and holy people are all pathways toward greater spiritual happiness. Some will scoff at religious believers, saying they are poor, deluded individuals. Rick Warren, author of *The Purpose-Driven Life*, says, "I don't have enough faith to be an atheist." Don't be impressed by nonbelieving scoffers who claim they are better off not to believe. They are clearly wrong. Find your own combination of spiritual practices and religious communities, and follow it. Be involved, be committed, and be loyal to your religious or spiritual path. Your happiness will follow.

Chapter 13
Epigenetics

Deuteronomy 5:
8 Thou shalt not make thee any graven image, or any likeness of any thing that is in heaven above, or that is in the earth beneath, or that is in the waters beneath the earth:
9 Thou shalt not bow down thyself unto them, nor serve them: for I the LORD thy God am a jealous God, visiting the iniquity of the fathers upon the children unto the third and fourth generation of them that hate me,
10 And shewing mercy unto thousands of them that love me and keep my commandments.

What is this business of the third and fourth generation suffering? It didn't make much sense to me until I started learning about epigenetics. What does that mean? Simply that the genome, the DNA that supposedly makes us who and what we are, doesn't explain all of the picture.

It turns out that there are certain things that can influence the third and fourth generation, something to do with *gene expression*. That means that just because we have a gene doesn't mean it will be active. It might be expressed, or it might be suppressed. The environment plays a weighty role in gene expression. Thus we shape our environment, but we are also shaped by the environment. We are influenced by what we influence.

The newest data suggest that under specific conditions, we pass on to our children which genes are expressed or suppressed. While this information is very new, it opens up exciting possibilities. I am going to argue that there might be ways that we can pass higher levels of happiness on to our great-grandchildren.

Swedes and Famine

Swedes keep very good records. Marcus Pembrey, a Professor of Clinical Genetics at the Institute of Child Health in London, and Swedish researcher Lars Olov Bygren, found evidence in these records of an environmental effect being passed down the generations. They have shown that a famine at critical times in the lives of the grandparents can affect the life expectancy of the grandchildren. This is the first evidence that an environmental effect can be inherited in humans.

The town of Overkalix near the Arctic circle had a famine in the 19th century, and because it was a very isolated area, there was no help from the outside. Pembrey and Bygren studied the health records of this small town and found some astonishing facts. It turns out that a century later, the effects of the famine are still being felt by the grandchildren.

A grandmother who suffered the effects of famine when she was pregnant and carrying a female will have granddaughters who die earlier. In other words, if the fetus suffered famine along with her mother, at a time when the eggs were developing in the ovaries, that effect would be felt one hundred years later.

Grandfathers also passed on effects. If a grandfather suffered famine when he was about to sexually mature, in late childhood going into adolescence, his grandsons would live longer. But if he had plenty to eat at those critical times, his grandsons would be more likely to suffer from diabetes.

So famine affected females and males almost in opposite ways, and both at the critical times when the gametes - the sperm and the eggs - were developing. The granddaughters died earlier, the grandsons lived longer. While that may not go on forever, the effect clearly does go to grandchildren and great-grandchildren.

How Does it Work?

Genes work by making specific proteins, the building blocks of our body. If you have blond hair, it is because the genes you received from your parents create a protein for your hair that is blond, not brunette. The old view of genetics was that these genes are given to us at birth, and they just carry out their instructions. If you have genes that contain a kind of time bomb for cancer, then at a certain time in your life, you develop that cancer. It's all in the genes.

Not so fast. Genes can be turned on or off. They can be *suppressed* with a kind of clamping molecule, or they can be *expressed* and allowed to do their work. The environment they live in has a great deal to do with which genes are expressed and which are suppressed.

That environment includes your own emotional state. When you are happy, your whole organism changes. And of course, when you are stressed, that changes your organism too. Now we know that creating that very environment changes gene expression and suppression! When you have a strong belief and faith in something, the body itself begins to change to match that belief. We have much more control over who we are than we would have ever thought.

Your Own Gene Expression

Recent research at Harvard found that if a person simply practices meditation for eight weeks (in this case, Herbert Benson's version of The Relaxation Response), the very genes themselves are changed. The body reacts less stressfully to outside events. We have always known that people who meditate were less reactive. We thought that was because the meditators have trained their brains not to react. They have tamed the wild amygdala, the stress-reactive center of the brain. There is no doubt that taming the amygdala plays a role.

But now we learn that the body itself is changing at a genetic level. Stress-reacting genes are suppressed, and calming genes are expressed. Some are clamped down, the ones that raise your cortisol and other stress hormones. Some are energized.

If you do meditate, and if you teach your children some kind of self-calming strategy, the effect will be lasting, perhaps even permanent.

What about Happiness?

So in the Bible it says that the third and fourth generation suffer from the sins of the parents. I suspect we are going to find that this provocative statement does hold up. The environment that we are in turns on and off some of our genes, and that will take several generations to resolve itself. Most importantly, part of this environment we live in is our own thoughts and beliefs. Belief, expectation, attitude have enduring effects on our own biology.

Let us end this book by speculating. What if your sons, around the time they become sexually mature, are in a very happy environment? What if those sons learn the keys, the true principles underlying a happy life? It is not unreasonable to think that the third and fourth generations will be blessed?

What if a daughter, during the time she is carried in the womb, is in a very happy environment? Her mother laughs a lot, feels good, and floods her own body with happiness hormones? It is likewise not unreasonable to wonder if the third and fourth generation of females from that little girl will carry happiness genes, or, speaking more accurately, the happiness genes will be expressed?

Of course these things are likely, but not certain. On the other hand, what do you have to lose? Practice happiness, teach your children happiness, make happiness a deliberate practice.

Start a family tradition today of high levels of happiness. Your grandchildren will rise up and call you blessed.

If you want to be happy for an hour, take a nap.
If you want to be happy for a day, go fishing.
If you want to be happy for three months, get married.
If you want to be happy for a year, inherit a lot of money.
But if you want to be happy for a lifetime, serve other people.
— Chinese saying

I have no greater joy than this, to hear about my children walking in truth.
3 John 1:4

References

Chapters 1 & 2
Seligman's *Learned Optimism* is where we learned about his dog experiments. Lyubomirsky's book, *The How of Happiness* is source of some of the optimism exercises.

Chapter 3
Byrne, A., & Byrne, D.G. 1993) The effect of exercise on depression, anxiety and other mood states : a review. *Journal of Psychosomatic Research, 37*, 6, 565-574. It says about what you'd expect, that exercise helps just about everything go better. Some other studies: Salmon, P. (2001) Effects of Physical Exercise on Anxiety, Depression, and Sensitivity to Stress: A Unifying Theory. *Clinical Psychology Review 21*, 33-61 argues that exercise works because it makes us less affected by stress. We cannot avoid stress, but we don't have to suffer because of it.

In an interesting study on the amount of exercise, Hansen CJ, Stevens LC, Coast JR (2001) Exercise Duration and Mood State: How Much is Enough to Feel Better? *Health Psychology 20*, 267-275 found that even ten minutes of exercise did raise the mood. They think that three ten minute episodes of exercise throughout the day may work best. Maybe you could run up and down stairs during your lunch hour. People who exercised twenty minutes were significantly better off. Thirty minutes was the same as twenty. Exercisers were less confused, less fatigued, and had more energy and vigor. And in a large survey study in Finland, "those who exercised at least twice a week reported higher levels of sense of coherence and a stronger feeling of social integration than their less frequently exercising counterparts." (Hassmen P, Koivula N, Uutela A, [2000]. Physical Exercise and Psychological Well-Being: A Population Study in Finland. *Preventive Medicine, 30*, 17-25.

Weightlifting also lifts mood, for example: Scully, D, Kremer, J Meade,

MM, Graham R. and Dudgeon, K (1998) Physical exercise and psychological well being: a critical review. *British Journal of Sports Medicine, 32*, 2, 111-120.

So basically the evidence is overwhelming. To be your best emotionally, you have to be better physically.

Chapter 4

Epictetus is worth reading. He left but a few notes, the *Enchridion* is where we read about his ideas on changing our own thinking. Google will lead you to several places where you can read it. I cannot give references on the part about detaching from thoughts since I formulated it myself, but I can tell you it works well.

ABCDE technique: Seligman's book, *Learned Optimism* has a good discussion of that tool.

Neutrality toward signs of fear: David Barlow is the researcher and clinician who pioneered this insight. There is much more on this topic that is beyond the scope of this book. Here are a couple of good interviews with him on this topic:

http://www.mentalhelp.net/poc/view_index.php?idx=119&d=1&w=9&e=349
http://www.apapractice.org/apo/insider/professional/conversations/barlow.html#

Chapter 4

Autogenic training is widely practiced in Europe, being a German invention. A large meta-analysis (an analysis of sixty studies on autogenic training) found that there are consistent positive results from the practice (Stetter & Kupper (2002). Autogenic training: a meta-analysis of clinical outcome studies. Applied Psychophysiology and Biofeedback 27(1):45-98.). I have practiced it for years and find it a wonderful quick solution to anxiety and stress.

Chapter 6

Again, David Barlow wrote about panic and fear and is a wonderful resource for professionals and the public. Anything by him is excellent.

Chapter 7
Some other good references: Thich Nhat Hahn's book *Anger: Wisdom for cooling the flames* is great, since he agrees with me. Another approach: Steve Stosny's book, *You Don't Have to Take It Anymore*. He emphasizes developing self-compassion and compassion for others. You can get my own book, *Get On The Peace Train: The journey from anger to harmony*. Order it directly from Head Acre Press, 166 East 5900 South, Ste. B-108, SLC, UT 84107.

Chapter 8
The Dalai Lama and Howard C. Cutler's book, *The Art of Happiness: A handbook for living* shows the Buddhist approach to compassion and forgiveness. From the Christian point of view, Everett Worthington's *The Power of Forgiving* is wise and deep. Forgiving makes us healthier: Witvliet, Charlotte vanOyen; Ludwig, Thomas E.; Vander Laan, Kelly L. (2001) Granting forgiveness or harboring grudges: Implications for emotion, physiology, and health. *Psychological Science*. Mar Vol 12(2) 117-123.

Chapter 9
Seligman found that when people identify their core strengths and try to energize them and put more emphasis on them, they do become happier. Simply doing that improved depressed patients as much as ordinary psychotherapy. Seligman, Rashid & Parks (2006) Positive Psychotherapy. *American Psychologist*, pp 774-788.
Haidt reported on his experiment in focusing on weakinesses at this address: http://faculty.virginia.edu/haidtlab/articles/strengths_analysis.doc

Chapter 10
Sonja Lyubomirsky reviews evidence that suggests that happy people have more connections, more successful marriages and friendships (Luybomirsky,

King & Diener (2005). The benefits of frequent positive affect: Does happiness lead to success? *Psychological Bulletin, 131*, 803-855.) She also argues that more connection therefore makes you happier in her book, *The How of Happiness* (2008, Penguin Press).

Chapter 11
Csikszentmihalyi has many articles and books. Read *Flow* for more background on this.
Buckingham and Clifton are authors of the book, *Now Discover Your Strengths*. They argue that basing the workplace on appreciation and enjoyment produces more productivity and loyalty to the organization than if the supervisor is critical and negative. They have a business oriented set of strengths and a test similar to the Values in Action test you took in Chapter 10.

Chapter 12
The 2008 Pew survey finds that around 95% of respondents do profess a belief in God. The 80% figure is from the 2008 Pew survey (Pew Forum.org) and Baylor surveys. The Baylor survey (http://www.baylormag.com/story.php?story=005980) is the source of the different views of God.

Chapter 13
Epigenetics: Wikipedia has a rather good overview of this area, and gives a history of the Swedish famine studies, but is full of difficult to understand scientific jargon. Here is a much easier account, and it seems to be accurate: http://www.hpathy.com/research/bhatia-miasms-epigenetics.asp
Also: http://www.pbs.org/wgbh/nova/transcripts/3413_genes.html
Take a look at the book, *The Biology of Belief* by Bruce H. Lipton. This scientist discusses how belief and the physical effect that belief has on our bodies can cause gene expression / suppression.